Living with
Green Power

A Gourmet Collection of
Living Food Recipes

Elysa Markowitz

Note to Readers: The information in this book is presented for educational purposes. It is not intended to replace the services of healing professionals for conditions that require them.

Instructions in this book are fully compatible with the new, advanced model Green Star machine.

Published by:

7432 Fraser Park Drive
Burnaby BC, Canada
V5J 5B9

Copyright © 1997

Cover Design: Terence Yeung, Shannon Taylor
Artwork: Raymond Cheung, Shannon Taylor
Recipe Photographs: Siegfried Gursche, Ron Crompton
Food styling: Elysa Markowitz

Hardcover
First Printing: February 1997
Second Printing: July 2000
Third Printing: May 2001
Fourth Printing: June 2002

Canadian Cataloguing in Publication Data

Markowitz, Elysa, 1947-
Living with green power

Includes index.
ISBN 0-920470-11-4

1. Vegetable juices. 2. Fruit juices. 3. Raw foods. I Title.
TX840. M5M37 1997   641.5'89   C97-910032-1

Printed and bound in Canada

Acknowledgements

There are a host of people I want to thank who helped me take this book from an idea to a reality. First and foremost, John Lysohir and Jae Choi for introducing me to the Green Power machine in the first place, and for sharing their friendship, knowledge and experience. Throughout our work together, these guys have just let me do what I do best - talk, prepare food and eat.

It was through Jae that I had the pleasure to meet Siegfried Gursche, Alive Books publisher and the man who made this book possible. With Jae's wife Jinhee and Siegfried's wife Christel, plus all the wonderful people I met while working trade shows and health conferences, my experiences over the last couple years working with the Green Power machine and culminating in this book have been fabulous.

Siegfried Gursche has been a special person to work with on this project. We both saw the need for a book that would show people just how many recipes can be prepared with this revolutionary machine. From our first talks in Las Vegas to our photo sessions for this book, Siegfried's enthusiasm for natural health and the Green Power machine has been contagious.

Our mutual love of photography made the photo sessions a delight! Siegfried and Ron Crompton, Alive photographer, understood that raw food must be seen, not just written about, to show its appeal. While working with these fellows, humor and patience abounded, and I thank both them and the Alive staff for all their help. Especially, Christine Olsen for helping prepare the food for the photographs, Zuzanna Krkoskova for shuttling me to and fro, and Sieglinde Janzen for her gracious hostessing. Most of all I would like to thank Alive chef Stephen Case. Meeting him was a total joy. I thank you Stephen for your tireless and enthusiastic energy and for sharing your creativity with both me and this project. My time spent at Alive was like being at a party where you go home feeling ready to do it all over again.

Also, I want to thank my good friend Kim Selbert, who was so generous and supportive of me having Green Power workshops at her home while staying there as a guest. We had fun making and eating the food, and sharing these times together. Good friends are invaluable.

Thanks go to Darrell Price, my friend and lover, who was helpful throughout this book's creation. While writing it, he fed me and rubbed my aching neck when I needed it most. He has supported me not only during this project, but also during my initial work with the Green Power machine at Dr. Cousens' center and when I had to take my work on the road. I could not have done it without you.

And, I want to thank my family for all their support. Their love and friendship means a lot to me. Family is an important foundation and I owe so much to mine for the love they shared with me all these years. Mom (in Heaven), Dad, Annie and Julie—thank you and I love you lots.

In closing, I want to thank God whose gentle spirit keeps me going day after day with the thought that I am doing good work by helping others eat better, take better care of themselves and better care of our planet. Life is about more than just food, but I do appreciate Mother Nature for all She shares with us. This project has been one from the heart, and I share it with all my readers with love.

Blessings to you all,
Elysa Markowitz

Table of Contents

Foreword

The Green Power machine* coupled with the living food lifestyle is like visiting a foreign country—it takes a tastebud adjustment period to truly settle in and savor the subtleties of unfamiliar textures or to appreciate the delicate interplay of natural flavors. Between the endpoints of introduction time and comfort zone lies a vast, virtually unexplored territory, until now.

In *Living with Green Power,* Elysa invites you for a friendly guided tour of the Green Power machine. You will learn how to assemble and disassemble it, why it is so unique and versatile and how this remarkable appliance can transform the otherwise culinary shock period into an easy and delicious transition. Who knows, you may even relax, put your feet up and read for awhile—I know, I did.

Living with Green Power commands a tribute with its array of fabulous recipes and good-enough-to-eat photographs. Ms. Markowitz has liberally spiced this book with nature's own vibrant art which welcome us to step right in and have fun creating raw food recipes that are great tasting and even better for your health.

I have spent time with Ms. Markowitz, watching her teach many of the delights in this book. She shares the secrets to the bountiful feast that results from her mastery of culinary arts and teaches us to release the creative chef within. This book is a personal extension of Ms. Markowitz's living food magic—right in your own home.

From juices and soups to appetizers and desserts royale, *Living with Green Power* offers a wide selection of gourmet recipes—frubets, seed cheeses, sauces, salsas, main dishes, parfaits and more. Or it can show you how to keep it simple with a bowl of hearty soup and whole grain crackers.

Living with Green Power is an international culinary excursion with amazing raw food recipes, humor, helpful hints and useful resources all along the way.

Bon appetite.

E. L. Waselus, M.D., Ph.D.
January 1997

* Instructions in this book are fully compatible with the new, advanced model Green Star machine.

Introduction

Congratulations. You have made a big step by picking up a book that could change your life. If you like to juice, this is the book for you. If you like to eat, then this will be a new adventure in eating. None of the foods in this book is cooked. The recipes are prepared with fruits, vegetables, nuts, seeds and grains. There are many labels that could be attached to this recipe book - vegetarian, vegan, whole foods, living foods, raw, natural, sugarless or cholesterol free. I feel the name "Nature's Best" sums them up. The food is not cooked, so you are getting all the vitamins, minerals and enzymes from the meals prepared in this book. Whether you want to drink or chew your food, these recipes will enhance your dining pleasure at any meal.

The ingredients for these recipes can be found at many markets and most natural food stores. Any ingredients you do not find can be located in the Food Resources section at the back of the book. All the recipes in this book are prepared with the Green Power machine - a machine that will improve your time in the kitchen. It did mine, and I want to tell you what it can do for you.

Yes, you can make these foods with other machines. I did before I tried the Green Power machine. I used blenders, food processors and other juicers. But, once the Green Power machine came into my life, most of the others left. I hardy ever use them now. This machine has given me a chance to play with my foods in ways I never dreamed. I hope it inspires you to do the same.

When I first heard about this machine, from John Lysohir and Jae Choi, I thought I did not need it. After all, I had all the major machines on the market and they did the trick, or so I thought. But, once I actually spent time using it, my mind was alive with the array of foods I could prepare, and the time I could save. Plus, there are other features that attracted me to this machine.

First of all, this machine makes practically no noise. After working long hours in the kitchen, this was reason enough for me. Sometimes, at a convention, I work all day with the Green Power machine on and, when I leave, I am not shell shocked from the noise. I can even talk on the phone and make juice at the same time. Also, it takes less time to make all the different kinds of juices. With other juicers I could not process wheatgrass and vegetables with the same machine. Green Power juices it all. Plus, the juice is free of pulp. In the past, I spent hours straining juice from other juicers. Now I do not have to strain the juice at all. The juice is clean and fresh. I have been able to juice greens, like kale or celery, without needing to use two machines, or worry about the juicer heating it into broth before I could drink it. And, the machine pulls the greens through effortlessly. The twin gears just grab the greens and pull them right in, no pushing required.

Getting even consistency with the nut and grain dishes I prepare was difficult with a food processor. The Green Power machine consistently makes the texture even, not lumpy. With other machines, I remember trying to add ingredients to a recipe after it is prepared and chunks or clumps of ingredients was the result. No problem, with the Green Power machine you can add an ingredient any time you like, and the texture of the food will always be the same - perfect.

I have never cut or nicked myself cleaning or assembling any of the parts for the Green Power machine, whereas I have with most other machines. With so many machine parts in my sink I would end up with bandaids all over my fingers. Not a problem with the twin gears as they are not sharp. In fact, the machine is completely user friendly. When I used to make a large quantity of food for workshops or parties, with a food processor, I would have to stop and make several batches, loading and unloading it with food to get more. This is not the case with the Green Power machine. I can keep making food until I get the right amount. Also, this is one of the few machines that can both juice and process whole foods. I can process fresh, frozen or dried foods individually or all together.

The Green Power machine works at 110 rpm, which means it applies a slow constant pressure to the food, as opposed to the masticating type of processors which tears into the food at 1,700 to 12,000 rpm, heats it up, and makes a lot of noise in the process.

Frozen fruit desserts are more fun to do with this machine than others because of the rice cake attachment. This nifty gadget sends out the fresh and frozen foods combined into tubes of colors and flavors. It is like having a professional dessert maker in your home.

Grains, bread sticks, pretzels and twisted breads are a delight to make with this machine. In the past, I worked for hours with hand operated grain mills, blenders and food processors, and had difficulties with all of them. But, grains go through a Green Power machine without a hitch.

Unlike other machines the Green Power machine uses magnetic technology to produce a focused magnetic field of 2600 gauss within the minute clearance of 4/1000th of an inch that aids in reconstructing the water molecules in the food or juice in order to magnetically extract more minerals from the produce and to carry those minerals within the foods' water structure. Thus, using magnetic technology is healthful to our bodies and extends the life of the food.

The book is organized into chapters: juices, blended drinks, frubet (pronounced frew-bay), soups made from fruits or vegetables, sauces from fruits or vegetables, dressings, supper ideas, grain dishes and desserts. You can put together your own meal planning menus, adding a dish or an entire meal from this book. Make meals that work best for you and your family. For optimum nutrition, add a salad with at least three different vegetables to most any meal.

Whatever recipes you choose, you are in for a treat. They are intended to inspire you to combine certain ingredients and there are endless possibilities. Use these recipes as a spring board, adding more of one ingredient, less of another. You might like more spices, or different ones. These recipes are not cast in stone. The purpose of this book is to help you understand how to use the Green Power machine and to learn the benefits of eating raw foods. As you play with the recipes, you will probably create new ones and new ways of using the machine. Go for it! I enjoy preparing food with the Green Power machine and I know you will too. With this enthusiasm to spur you on, go ahead and enjoy reaping the rewards of raw foods preparation.

Part I

About Raw Food Preparation

Chapter I
Getting Ready to Prepare the Food

Stocking your kitchen with useful tools makes any food preparation fun and easy. Finding them in your area, or when you travel can also be an adventure. So, whether your kitchen is fully stocked now, or you build-up your tools gradually, listed below are tools that will enhance your kitchen experience.

Cutting Board: One or two wood boards, various sizes.

Sharp Knives: Henckels or Japanese varieties are good quality. Find at least two knives, a paring knife (a smaller blade for slicing) and a chef's knife (a larger knife for chopping and fine dicing). Or, try a zirconia blade for a light weight blade that is very hard and rarely needs sharpening. (See Resources for supplier.)

Graters: Find one grater to do the standard grates and the other to Julienne. The Multi-slicer will slice and Julienne. I found a grater that has five sides or functions. It stands on its own and can slice, fine or coarse grate and zest citrus peel. Also, it has a covering that protects fingers and knuckles from scrapes. (See Resources section for more information on this grater.)

Glass Pie Plates: Pyrex is the best for making puddings or mousse, seed or nut cheeses and sorbet or fruit pies. It is also a lovely serving container for chips and dip.

Cookie Cutters: Not a must, but so much fun for making decorative foods. The best selection can be found at restaurant supply stores, Japanese markets and specialty kitchen stores. Have fun selecting your favorites.

Peeler: A sharp peeler can help take the wax off cucumbers or apples. Unless you have a wax deficiency, your body cannot digest the wax so it is healthier peel it off. Better yet, buy unwaxed fruits and vegetables.

Wooden, Glass or Stainless Steel Mixing Bowls: These substances are friendly to the foods you will be preparing. Plastic gives off chemicals and should be avoided.

Wide Mouthed and Lidded Glass Jars: Glass is your best bet for soaking, germinating, sprouting and fermenting. Also, wide mouthed jars are easier to get ingredients in and out.

Essential Raw Food Kitchen Equipment

Although this book focuses on the Green Star machine, here are some other kitchen appliances helpful when preparing the recipes in this book.

Blender: This is a lower priced choice than industrial strength blenders though not as efficient, but certainly suited for beginners. There is a bartender version available that is more powerful than the regular version. Look for these in department stores or discount warehouse type stores. Useful for dips, sauces, frostings and quick blending.

Industrial Strength Blender: I recommend two "industrial strength" blenders, one is the Vita-Mix and the other is the K Tec blender. Both are capable of high speed, high power blending. (See resource section for purchasing information.) Excellent for sauces, salsas, soups, dips, cookie and bread dough, smoothies and sorbet.

Nut and Seed Grinder (also called a coffee bean grinder): Mainly used to powder spices, seeds or nuts. (Nuts and seeds need to be soaked and sun dried or dehydrated to grind, otherwise they turn to mush.)

Excalibur Dehydrator: For most people a nine tray model is practical. This size has the greatest versatility for making dehydrated breads, crackers, cookies, dried or baked fruits and vegetables, fruit rolls or crêpes and puddings. The trays can be added or removed to allow for the space needed for pie dishes or flat crackers/cookies. Modular spacing is an option you want in a dehydrator, plus this dehydrator blows air across the food, not from bottom to top, which overheats the lowest tray. With the

Excalibur, the food on all the trays is equally dehydrated. Make sure to order the reusable teflex sheets, they make dehydrating liquid recipes a breeze.

Stove Top Equipment: You can use several options to heat on top of an electric or gas stove. A double boiler heats the water below and you can check how warm your food is getting by tasting often, or using your built-in thermometer —your finger. Another option is to warm a skillet on the stove top, turn off the heat or take the pan off the burner then add the food and place the pan on and off the heat as needed only to warm. This procedure takes a bit of practice and careful attention. Keeping the temperature at or below 110°F (45°C) preserves the vital enzymes.

About these Living Food Recipes

When I was first introduced to the Green Power Machine, I was making the food for Dr. Cousens' health center in Arizona. Dr. Cousens had a living foods diet at his center. This means that we did not cook too many of the foods at any given meal. Plus, there were guests who were juice fasting and we would prepare the juice.

The Green Power machine made preparing these meals much easier and got me thinking about how many more dishes I could prepare with this invention. Since then, the more I have experimented with it, the more I marvel at its ability to help me prepare better foods in less time and I have been impressed with its versatility. To be able to both juice and process whole foods has been a real benefit. Whether I want to use fruits, vegetables, nuts, seeds or grains, I now have the machine that can prepare them all.

The following recipes describe the different foods this machine can prepare, without cooking them; how to juice, blend, homogenize and texturize foods into great meals. Also, these recipes are handy when you just do not want to cook or when you want to enjoy a different flavor of food by not cooking it. But, you can always warm up your Green Powered foods.

For some folks, the recipes will introduce them to a myriad of choices on how to prepare foods you already eat, but are used to cooking. For others, it will offer creative ideas of what to eat. Hopefully, these recipes will inspire you to broaden your meal planning horizons.

Often, I begin my day with fresh juice. Or, I will have a blended morning drink which offers me the choice of using whole food and juice mixed. For lunch and dinner, I love to eat soup and salads. The dips with vegetable or fruit chips are a healthy snacking choice. Soups from juices, whether from fruits or vegetables, are so refreshing. These soups are cooling for long hot days. In the winter, when the mornings and evenings cool down, the soups can be warmed in the electric skillet or on the stove, keeping a careful watch not to overheat them and destroy the enzymes, vitamins and minerals. The main course dishes are fun to make because you can eat them raw, warmed or dehydrated, or store them and have food to eat later in the week when you are busy. Unlike most prepared foods, the Green Power machine's technology helps the food you prepare and store stay fresh longer.

I confess, I do not eat a raw food diet all the time. There are times when I eat cooked food. But, a diet higher in cooked foods, particularly cooked starches and carbohydrates, can cause people to gain weight. From my own experience I know that restricting my diet to raw food is the easiest way to stay healthy and maintain weight. When I was eating a diet rich with living foods, I actually ate more food but stayed thin. Also, I had more energy and my body ached less.

The point is to eat what makes you feel best, or better. There is a balance we all have to find for ourselves. No one can tell us what makes us feel good or creates health for us individually. Combine the recipes in this book with other favorites and enjoy learning how to prepare living foods. After you have been eating Green Powered foods, see how you feel. Has a health problem cleared up? Have you lost weight? Take the time and invest in your health.

There are many books written about the functions and benefits enzymes. Two of the best books are included in the Bibliography. What is important about enzymes is that we need them for most of our bodily functions from digestion, assimilation to elimination. When we eat raw food, the enzymes to help digest it are found in the food. The more we cook our food, the more we destroy its enzymes and need to use our own resources, our own savings account of enzymes. Ever notice how tired you feel after a rich cooked meal, such as Thanksgiving dinner? Usually, you want to lie down and relax for hours. Your system is trying to digest the food and it takes all your energy and your production of enzymes to do so. I was amazed to learn that the process of digestion can take up between 40% to 60% of the energy from the food we eat, just to digest it. In fact, research has been done that clearly demonstrates the difference in diet, age and our enzyme levels. The research showed that the average saliva of a 20 year old had much higher enzyme levels than a 69 year old, as much as 30 times more in the younger person. This shortage of enzymes can be reversed by eating more living foods full of enzymes and not using up your enzyme saving account. Certainly I have felt a difference in my health and energy since adding more living foods to my diet, and so can you.

Some of the recipes in the book require soaking the nuts, seeds or grains. This is for two reasons. One reason is to remove any enzyme inhibitors that block the digestion of the food. The other reason is to soften the food making it easier to chew and digest (and easier for the machine to process). A food that has germinated, been soaked and rinsed, has started a biological change. This change creates a new food, a seed. Usually food in a germinating and sprouting state are richer in complex carbohydrates and are easier to digest. They are a living food, not just a raw food. They would grow into a plant if you put them in soil. Sprouting is the next step in the germinating process. A seed has sprouted when you can see a shoot forming. Sunflower seeds form a shoot after a short amount of soaking time, but they get bitter quickly. Try to soak only what you plan to eat to avoid any unwanted sprouting or taste variations. Rinse the sprouts and use them that day. If you want more sprouts, soak only as much as you need.

Balance seems to be the key to health. Finding your own balance in health and nutrition is what this book can help you do. Now, you can prepare a wider range of living food year round, warm or cold weather.

Measurements and Quantities

Recipes are not an exact science. This is an attempt to give amounts and translate measurements into metric.

Liquid and Dry Measure Equivalences			Food Quantity Measurement		
American System		**Metric**			
1/4 teaspoon	=	1.25 milliliters	Apple: 1 medium	=	1 cup, chopped
1/2 teaspoon	=	2.5 milliliters	Avocado: 1 medium	=	1 cup, mashed
1 teaspoon	=	5 milliliters	Banana: 1 medium	=	3/4 cup, sliced
1 tablespoon	=	15 milliliters	Bell pepper: 1 medium=		3/4 cup, diced
1/3 cup	=	80 milliliters	Broccoli: 1 stalk	=	2 cups (stalk and flowers)
1/2 cup	=	120 milliliters	Cabbage: 1	=	25 cups, minced
1 cup	=	240 milliliters	Carrots: 2 medium	=	1 cup, diced
1 pint	=	(2 cups or	Celery: 3 stalks	=	1 cup, diced
	=	480 milliliters)	Lemon: 1 medium	=	2 tablespoons juice
					and 1 tablespoon grated peel
1 quart	=	(4 cups or	Mango: 1 medium	=	1 cup, peeled and cubed
	=	960 milliliters/32 ounces)	Onion: 1 medium	=	1 cup, diced
			Orange: 1 medium	=	1/2 cup juice
1 gallon	=	(4 quarts or	Parsley: 1 bunch	=	3-1/2 cups, chopped
	=	3.84 liters)	Pineapple: 1 medium	=	4 cups, peeled and cubed
			Tomato: 1 medium	=	3/4 cup, diced

Time to Go Shopping

Knowing what to have on hand makes menu planning more fun and less annoying when you are only missing one ingredient. Although, being short an ingredient is sometimes how new recipes are created.

Buying organic is the first suggestion. You have heard me suggest this already. It is still the healthiest rule when buying any kind of food.

Here are some simple suggestions of spices and foods to stock your pantry with so you can make meals in minutes:

Storing the staples

Store nuts, seeds, beans and grains in glass to help the food stay fresh longer. Keeping them in a dark, cool place enhances their shelf-life even further.

Spices

- ❑ allspice
- ❑ basil
- ❑ turmeric
- ❑ cayenne
- ❑ cinnamon
- ❑ cilantro
- ❑ cumin
- ❑ dill
- ❑ caraway seeds
- ❑ parsley (fresh or dried)
- ❑ poultry spice
- ❑ garlic (fresh cloves or granulated)
- ❑ Mexican spice blend
- ❑ miso (a fermented soy bean paste for soup broth)
- ❑ nutmeg (the whole seed is tastiest grated fresh)
- ❑ onion (flakes or Onion Magic)
- ❑ vanilla (the non-alcoholic variety)
- ❑ Celtic salt and/or soy seasoning (shoyu, wheat-free tamari or Bragg's)

Nuts

- ❑ almonds
- ❑ cashews
- ❑ hazelnuts (filberts)
- ❑ pecans
- ❑ pinenuts
- ❑ walnuts

Seeds

- ❑ flax
- ❑ sunflower
- ❑ sesame
- ❑ pumpkin

Dried Fruits

- ❑ apricots (Turkish are my favorite)
- ❑ currants
- ❑ dates
- ❑ mango
- ❑ papaya
- ❑ pineapple
- ❑ peaches
- ❑ raisins or your favorites

Grains

- ❑ barley
- ❑ kamut
- ❑ oats
- ❑ rye
- ❑ wheat

Fruits

Keep fresh fruits that are in season. And, keep a bunch of bananas on hands for either freezing or smoothies. I like to keep apples and oranges around almost year round, as well as avocados and tomatoes (dried and fresh).

Fresh Vegetables

- ❑ carrots
- ❑ celery
- ❑ baby greens
- ❑ cucumber
- ❑ cabbage
- ❑ lettuce (romaine, red, leaf, butter, red oak) plus your favorites

Sprouts

- ❑ alfalfa
- ❑ clover
- ❑ sunflower

Sea Vegetables

- ❑ dulse
- ❑ kelp
- ❑ nori sheets

I find as long as I have supplies on hand, I eat healthier food. Whatever threatens to go bad, I juice, dehydrate or freeze. Keeping soaked nuts, seeds, beans and grains readily available gives me more options for recipes and snacks.

Do not go out and buy everything on this list all at once. First clear your kitchen out of those white sugar, white flour and processed items to make room for the good stuff. Get a few items from each category. Let it be an adventure to create a new kitchen, with better food choices in it for you and your family. Find a farmers market. Find stores that you enjoy shopping in and let the transition to healthy eating be a pleasure.

Chapter II
About the Green Star Machine

This section shows you how to use the parts of the Green Star machine and its predecessor, the Green Power. The Green Star has a sleek new design and looks slightly smaller, although both machines have the same functional parts. If you are like me, you like to see the features, not just read about them. So, this section includes color photographs to help you understand the inner workings of the machines. After reading this chapter, nothing can hold you back from making delicious, nutritious Green juices and raw food for your friends and family.

Each quiet juicer and food processor is seven machines in one—a regular juicer for fruits, vegetables and greens, a wheatgrass juicer, a nut butter maker, a baby food maker (from whole, dried, fresh or frozen foods), a sorbet or frozen fruit maker, a pasta maker and a rice cake (mochi) maker.

The Green Power and Green Star machines, made in Korea, are known worldwide for producing superior nutritional quality juice and for their award winning ability to perform above and beyond the capacity of yesterday's centrifugal and masticating juicers. Some of the prestigious awards won by Green Power include: Silver Medal in the category of Best Equipment from *alive* Award of Excellence, 1999; Grand Prize winner at the 9th International Invention/New Products Exhibition in Pittsburgh, USA in May 1993; Silver Medal

winner at the International Exhibition of Inventions in Nürnburg, Germany in March 1993; winner of the Korean President's 1st Prize Invention Day in May 1993 and Silver Medal winner at the 20th International Exhibition of Inventions in Geneva, Switzerland also in May 1993.

In addition to its modern appearance, its revolutionary design incorporates twin helical gears which slowly rotate at 110 RPM, (no blades, rotors or augers) triturating (grinding, mashing and compressing) the raw produce, expelling it, and juicing or homogenizing it. These twin gears feature a pocket-recessed area to more easily accept fibrous vegetables and herbs, three separate points that cut strong fibers such as celery so that the appliance does not get jammed or clogged. Masticating juicers like the Champion tear into the food at 1,725 RPM (15 times faster), while the Norwalk blade spins at 3,250 RPM (29 times faster). This spinning speed creates heat which destroys vital enzymes. The Green Power's and Green Star's 110 revolutions per minute creates a minimal heat build up in the juice and therefore initial oxidation is delayed allowing the juice to stay fresh longer.

A recent independent comparative study on how five different juicers affect juice stability showed that apples at 59.9°F juiced in a Green Power only increased in temperature a bit over half of one degree to 60.44°F. The other juicers ranged from almost 3-1/2 degrees to over 14 degrees higher than the original temperature of the fruit.

According to a tape put out by Green Power International:

"Recently, independent nutritional testing on juicers and fresh squeezed juice has resulted in some pretty surprising and impressive information. In that test, 2.4 pounds of vegetable greens consisting of celery, parsley, kale, swiss chard and sunflower sprouts produced 20 ounces of juice using a nationally recognized brand of masticating juicer. Another juicer (the Green Power) in that test yielded 26.67 ounces—that is

25% more juice from the same quantity and proportion of greens. Analyzing the mineral content of the juice by volume obtained in that testing revealed significant differences also. From the same juicer that produced more juice (the Green Power) came 95.4% more calcium, 173.5% more iron, 96.95% more magnesium, 61.4% more potassium, 205% more silicon, 108.2% more zinc. In the 19 minerals tested over 68.98% more.

The twin gears with the extremely close clearance of 4/1000ths of an inch, employ another technology that is revolutionizing the juicing and food processing industry—magnetic and far infrared properties. Today, we are seeing magnetic technology enter our lives in many different ways: magnetic beds, cleaning products, toothbrushes, jewelry and even devices that generate pulsating magnetic fields to energize or relax us.

With the Green Power machine, this technology has entered into the food processing arena. For at the cores of each of the twin gears is a series of in line magnets equaling 2600 gauss. Plus, a bioceramic generated far infrared, also known as life force frequencies. Far infrared, according to the information issued from Tribest: "is the natural resonant frequency range of water and organic substances including man. We call it the life force frequency. Infrared wave length ranges from .7 to 1000 microns just beyond visible light. Far infrared is a part of this wave length family we use in infrared photography, mapping the earth's surface and guiding missiles to their target. Our skin radiates 9.36 microns far infrared wave which is very close to the resonant frequency of a water molecule—and rightly so since our bodies are about 70% water. Far infrared waves are the safest and most beneficial energy source available."

Green Power places a specially formulated bioceramic material around the in line magnets at the core of each twin gear. The bioceramic compound uses the mechanical energy from the turning of the twin gears to not only generate far infrared energy, but also to radiate it, thus further stabilizing the fragile structure of the juice."

From my understanding of the process: as the food to be processed flows through the focused field, the water molecules are broken up allowing the atoms to recombine with other minerals such as calcium, potassium, sodium and magnesium into new molecular structures. This magnetic process therefore extracts a greater percentage of mineral nutrients from the produce during juice extraction and is instrumental in keeping those minerals in a suspended colodial form the body can use for a longer length of time.

Green Power offers the features I have been searching for in a food processing machine. One of my friends calls it the "more machine"—the more she asks of it, the more she likes it. I have found the same to be true. The more I use it, the more I enjoy using it.

The Green Power and Green Star machines are energy efficient, operating at 190 watts with 1/4 horsepower, while most blenders start working at 250 watts.

Let us look at the Green Power machine, part by part and discuss their various functions.

Standard Parts:

Outlet adjusting knob: This knob functions in two ways. When the machine is juicing, it adjusts the flow of the output, regulating the amount of juice in the pulp. If you want drier pulp, tighten this knob. If the pulp or foam backs up in the feeding chute, loosen this knob and release the pulp. The other use for this knob is to stop any flow out the front end of the machine, directing the food out to one exit place, the juice outlet. In this use, the knob is screwed securely into place.

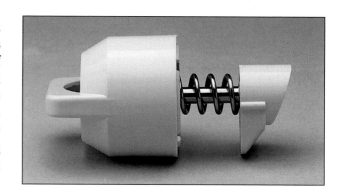

Pulp discharge casing: (pulp discharge outlet) Located at the front end of the machine, this is where the pulp from the juice is expelled. The rate of flow from this outlet is determined by the position of the outlet adjusting knob. When the knob is fully tightened, no pulp will exit this outlet. As the knob is loosened, pulp can be pushed out. The more it is loosened, the wetter the pulp will be.

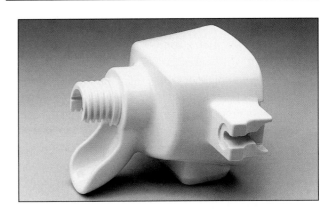

Screens and blanks: The Green Power and Green Star machine comes with two screens and two blanks to be described in the next section.

Fine screen: Used for juicing. This screen provides maximum juice extraction and pulp separation. It is used for most juicing needs.

Coarse screen: Used for juicing, when more fiber is desired in juice. This screen allows some pulp to mix with the juice. Can be used for softer fruits and vegetables.

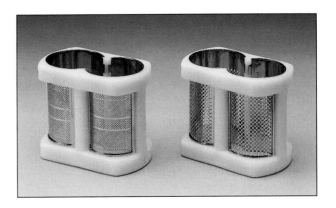

Open blank or homogenizing blank:
(Official name used in Green Power manual.) Used for coarser homogenizing of whole foods. This can be used for processing any whole foods such as fruits, vegetables, nuts, grains and seeds. It produces a coarser blending of the harder foods. It allows the food to drop out the juice outlet, when the outlet adjusting knob is securely in place. It can be used for making baby foods, sorbet, frubets, nut or vegetable patés or loafs, crunchy nut butters and coarse grain blends for crackers.

Closed blank:
(Official name used in Green Power manual.) Used for finer homogenizing of whole foods. This part is best used when you want to push the food out the pulp discharge outlet, or want a finer blending of whole foods fresh, dried or frozen. When the rice cake guide is in place, the machine will push the food out through this opening, making bread sticks, pretzels or fun sorbet swirls. Useful for sorbet, finer nut butters, smoother fruit or vegetable sauces and patés or loafs.

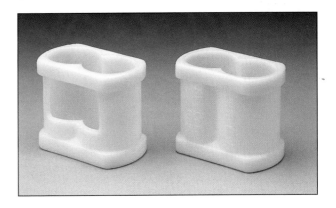

Twin gears: The two stainless steel gears rotate at 110 RPM, and are covered with a special polymer named Acetal on the tips that is non-reactive to any acids from vegetable or fruit juices. Inside each gear is a series of in-line magnets, surrounded by bioceramic particles, part of far infrared technology. The magnets work in conjunction with these bioceramic particles and produce a magnetic field of 2,600 gauss within a minute clearance of 4/1000ths of an inch. As the food passes over this magnetic field the water molecules are reconstructed to magnetically extract more minerals from the produce and to carry those minerals within the juice or food's water structure, keeping the food or juice stable longer. When putting the twin gears in position, be sure to match up the dots. The "female" side (drive gear) has two dots, with a space in between them. The "male" side (free wheel gear) has one dot that fits in between the "female" dots.

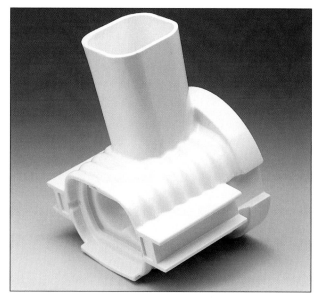

Twin gears housing: This housing slides easily onto two tracks (right and left sides) and keeps the twin gears and screen in place. The latching arms open and close at the end with the knobs (opening - left loose, closing - right tight), and must be securely tightened for the machine to properly function. Be aware that these knobs can and will screw off entirely. They will screw back on, but it is important not to misplace them. When disassembling the machine, the latching arms must be opened to allow the twin gears housing to slide off its tracks.

Feeding chute: ① This is where you put the food to be processed. Be sure to cut the food so it fits easily through the opening.

Body: ② (motor inside) Be sure not to put this part of the machine into water. It houses the motor and must be kept dry. A moist cloth or towel will clean off the exterior, so rinsing or submerging in water are not necessary.

Lifting (convenience) handle: ③ This convenient design feature allows this 19 pound machine to be carried and lifted with greater ease.

Power switch: ④ This switch has two functions. First, it will turn the machine on and off. Second, it has a reverse position that will unstick any food caught in the gears. Should the machine stop for any reason, just flick this switch downward, and the gears will move in the reverse direction. This usually removes any caught food. Then, to start the machine again just flick the switch back to the upward position.

Power cord storage compartment: ⑤ No unsightly cords need ever dangle from this machine. Tucking the power cord away in the storage compartment allows for a tidier look when traveling or when finished using the machine.

Safety tray: ⑥ This is used to help guide the food down the feeding chute, and it should be in place whenever the plastic or wooden plungers are used. It snaps downward into place, with the arrow pointing toward the handle.

Optional Available Parts:

Rice cake guide: This attachment funnels food out the pulp discharge outlet in a tubular shape, perfect for serving sorbet, bread sticks or pretzels. (with closed blank)

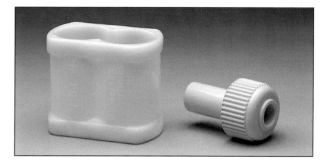

Pasta output attachment:
The Green Star attachment makes two different types of pasta: spaghetti and fettuccini. Rotate the attachment to make the type of pasta desired. The Green Power's attachment makes three types of pasta.

Pasta guide and pasta screw: The pasta guide holds the pasta screw. The pasta screw is used instead of the twin gears. The twin gears are removed, and the pasta screw, inside the pasta guide, is put into the machine, with the pasta output attachment set to the type of pasta desired.

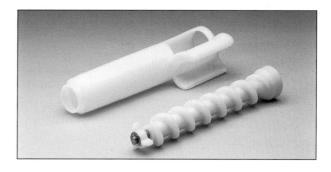

Glass juice pitcher: (Juice bowl) Putting fresh juice in glass is always recommended. Pour this pitcher slowly to avoid unwanted spilling. See picture page 10.

Drip tray: This feature of the Green Power and Green Star catches the food coming out the pulp discharge outlet and prevents the food from spilling onto the counter.

Wooden and plastic plungers: These handy plungers help push the food through the feeding chute. Be sure to use them with the safety tray in position on top of the feeding chute. Remember to take out the plunger when the machine is on and there is no food in the feeding chute. The plastic plunger should not be used like a piston, but should be used with consistent, gradual downward pressure. The arrows on the side of the plunger direct you to point the plunger toward the front of the machine. Pumping the plunger can produce unnecessary foam, and compact materials that would otherwise flow through the feeding chute by themselves.

Cleaning brush: This helps clean the machine's hard to reach places.

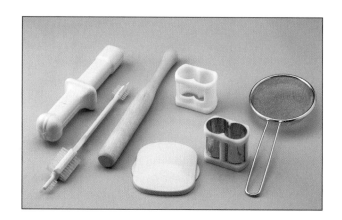

The operating manual provides instructions on how to take apart and reassemble your machine. The following steps help describe what part to use when:

For vegetable and fruit juice:

To assemble the machine for juicing:

1. First slide the twin gears housing on the tracks on the body.

2. Take the twin gears and match the dots (the single dot on the "male" gear fits inside of the pair of dots on the "female" gear). Slide the gears into their slots, twisting gently and pressing into place.

3. Slide the fine screen over the end of the gears.

4. Slide the pulp discharge casing over screen and bring both latching arms into place, tightening the latching arm knobs securely. There shouldn't be space between the twin gears housing and the body of the machine.

5. Screw in the outlet adjusting knob, not too tight, to allow the pulp to exit the pulp discharge outlet.

6. Place the tray and the glass pitcher under the juice outlet.

7. Put a bowl under the pulp discharge outlet to catch the pulp.

8. Begin juicing.

For vegetable or fruit sauces, coarser blended grains or nuts, nut butters, nut loafs, patés, baby food, frubets or sorbet:

1. To assemble the machine for homogenizing, first slide the twin gears housing on the tracks on the body.

2. Take the twin gears and match the dots (the single dot on the "male" gear fits inside the pair of dots on the "female" gear). Slide gears into their slots, twisting gently and pressing into place.

3. Slide the open blank or homogenizing blank over the end of the gears, thin panel toward the front. This is the only screen that has to be put in a certain way. If the thick side is toward the front, it blocks some of the flow of the food exiting the outlet machine.

4. Slide pulp discharge casing over screen and bring both latching arms into place, tightening the latching arm knobs securely. There should not be any space between the twin gears housing and the body of the machine.

5. Screw in the outlet adjusting knob, tightly. (Note: this is an optional step. If the knob is not put in place, the food will come out the pulp discharge outlet as well as the juice outlet. If this is preferred, be sure the bowl underneath is large enough to catch the food from both outlets.)

6. Put a bowl under the juice outlet, to catch the food. If the outlet adjusting knob is in place, nothing should come out the pulp discharge outlet.

For finer blended grains or nuts, nut butters, nut loaves, patés, baby food, frubet or sorbet:

There are two preparation method: Either the food can come out the pulp discharge outlet or it can by sculpted by using the rice cake guide.

1. To assemble the machine for homogenizing, first slide the twin gears housing on the tracks on the body.

2. Take the twin gears and match the dots (the single dot on the "male" gear fits inside of the pair of dots on the "female" gear). Slide the gears into their slots, twisting gently and pressing into place.

3. Slide the closed blank (rice cake attachment) over the end of the gears.

4. Slide the pulp discharge casing over the blank and bring the latching arms into place, tightening the latching arm knobs securely. There should not be any space between the twin gears housing and the body of the machine.

5. Optional: screw in the rice cake guide, tightly.

6. Put a bowl under the pulp discharge outlet or the rice cake guide opening, to catch the food. If you are using the closed blank (rice cake attachment), nothing should come out the juice outlet.

For making pasta:

1. To assemble the machine for making pasta, first slide the twin gears housing on the tracks on the body.

2. Take pasta screw and insert it into the pasta guide. Instead of using the twin gears, slide the pasta guide into the twin gears housing, twisting gently and pressing into place.

3. Select the type of pasta on the pasta output attachment then slide the attachment over the end of the pasta guide, and bring both of the latching arms into place, tightening the latching arm knobs securely. There should not be any space between the twin gears housing and the body of the machine.

4. Put a bowl under the pasta attachment to catch the food.

Cleaning Tips

Cleaning the Green Power machine is a breeze. A friend of mine told me that the first time he cleaned his machine he timed himself, expecting it to take half an hour or so. It took him seven minutes, and he was a beginner. I have been using the machine for over a year, and I can take it apart, wash it and reassemble it again in five minutes.

Note: Do not put any parts of the machine into the dishwasher.

The Green Power machine is so easy to clean because its features were built with convenience in mind. First, the parts slide easily on and off. Second, there are no sharp blades or parts to cut your fingers.

Here are some suggestions on how to make cleaning quick and efficient:

1. To remove stubborn stains, such as carrot juice, before taking apart the machine, alternate putting some of the carrot pulp with granulated white sugar through the feeding chute and over the twin gears. This gives the twin gears a quick shine.

   Or, run soaked almonds through the machine with the open or closed blank to bring the whiteness back to the tip of the gears. Really stubborn stains can be whitened by soaking the gears in white wine vinegar.

2. Rinse with cool water first before taking apart the machine. With the machine turned on, pour water down the feeding chute. Place a large bowl under the machine to catch the water from the lower and front end openings.

3. Take the machine apart as soon as the food processing is finished, and soak the parts in warm or cool water. Do not put the parts in the dishwasher.

4. Put a bowl or the empty pitcher under the area where the twin gears are attached to the machine, and splash the gears with water. This is the simplest and quickest way to clean this area. I like to use a nasal syringe or glass to splash water on this part. Food often gets stuck here after the rest of the parts have been removed. The cleaning brush and water can be used for those difficult or sticky foods such as grains and nuts, but leave a bowl underneath to catch any droppings.

5. A chopstick or other narrow tool works well to push food through the pulp discharge outlet.

Trouble Shooting
(If this happens, then try this...)

If: The machine does not start...
Then: if its an older model, check to see if the safety key is in place. For the newer models, check if the machine is plugged into a live outlet and check the fuse.

If: The twin gears are noisy...
Then: check to see if the twin gears are correctly aligned and that there are no hard materials or foreign objects between the gears.

If: The pulp discharge casing does not fit properly...
Then: the left hand twin gear may not be seated correctly. Give it a twist and push it further into position.

If: The pulp discharge casing begins shaking...
Then: check that the latching arm knobs are tight and secure.

If: The pulp is not being ejected...
Then: loosen the outlet adjusting knob.

If: There is too much pulp...
Then: tighten the outlet adjusting knob.

If: Pulp comes out with juice...
Then: check to see if the screen is in the proper position or loosen the outlet adjusting knob.

If: Not that much juice is expelled...
Then: check to see if the pitcher is under the juice outlet or if the outlet adjusting knob is secure.

If: Food is stuck in the feeding chute...

Then: turn off the machine and pull out the food. Restart machine and press down with the plunger to clear any remains from the chute. If this is not possible, turn off the machine, take it apart and clear the blockage. To avoid further problems of this sort, cut the food into smaller pieces and put it in slowly. Finish processing each batch before adding more food.

If: The machine stops or the twin gears are not able to move...

Then: turn the machine switch off and then down, to reverse. Restart and this should get the machine or the gears working again.

With these helpful hints in mind, you are on your way to a successful experience with your Green Star or Green Power machine. Read on for exciting raw food recipe ideas that will delight your tummy and your taste buds.

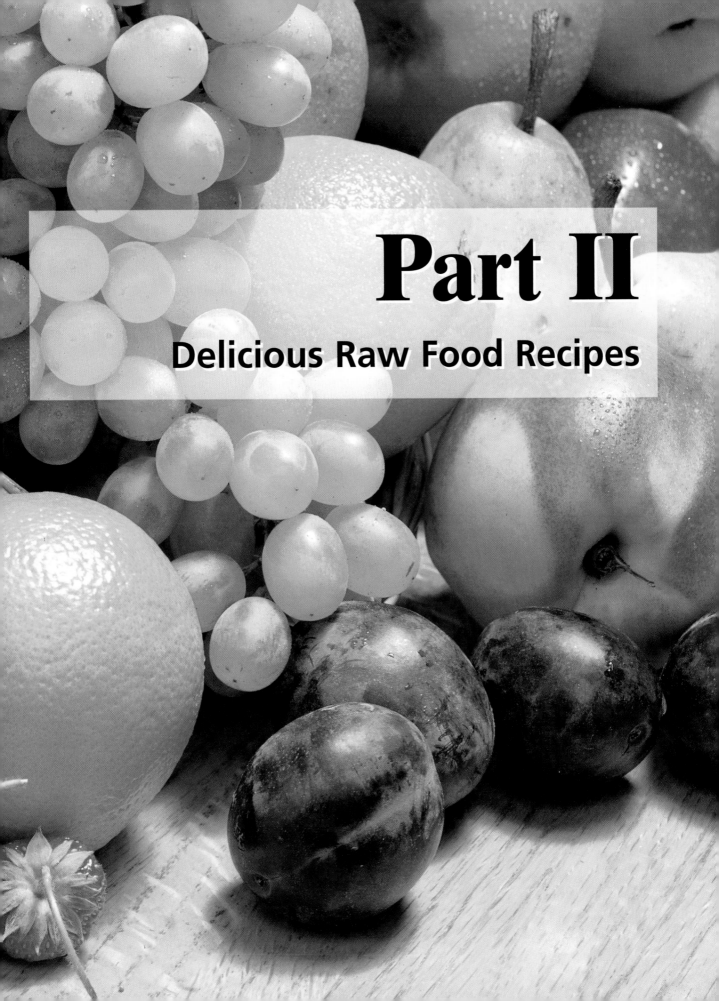

Part II
Delicious Raw Food Recipes

Chapter III
Juicy Juices

This section is filled with juice recipes that you can enjoy year round. First find the fruits and vegetables that are in season in your area. In-season produce will give you what your body needs for that time period. Look for the different varieties available in your area.

When you shop for produce, try to buy organic. Organic fruits and vegetables grow from a tiny seed, take only the earth's provisions (sun, water and soil) and give us food full of natural vitamins, minerals and flavor. The other reason to buy organic is that pesticides found on regular produce are toxic. There are safer solutions to the bug problem without resorting to noxious chemicals. So, if your produce is not organic, wash it thoroughly and avoid juicing its rind as it is full of pesticides.

Farmers markets are a wonderful choice for buying organic produce. To find markets in your area, check your local papers. You might have to travel a bit to find organic produce, but it is worth the trip. Starting a co-operative buying group is another way to get fresh organic produce. Better yet, grow your own organic produce. Plants and herbs grow in pots and small gardens can be created in any yard. Sprouts can be grown in any kitchen. Add sprouts to any of the vegetable juice recipes listed. Alfalfa or clover sprouts are easily mixed with most any juice.

Juicing produces a separation between the fiber and liquid content or juice. That fiber or pulp has a variety of uses. If you have animals, cats, dogs or other pets, the pulp from the vegetable juices is a wonderful addition to their dry food. I mix my leftover pulp in with the dry food, add warm water and other leftovers, and my pets love it. So do the chickens. I put extras in the compost bucket and feed it to them in the yard. There are other uses for the pulp. Some of it can be put around plants, to make a mulch. Also, it can be used as stuffing. Look in Chapter IX – What's for Supper for the Beyond Tuna recipe. If you bake, there are muffin and cake recipes that would be enhanced by using pulp as an ingredient.

Many books have been written about the effects of juicing. I have included some of the benefits in my Ingredient Information sections, but research, experiment and find what you need to know about juicing. The experience of juicing itself will teach you a lot about how to regain or maintain your health.

Begin by putting the Green Power machine on your counter. You will use it more when you can easily get to it. Then, juice more than you need. These juices will keep fresh for up to 24 hours, and some taste great even after 36 hours. For a longer lasting juice, with any of the recipes using apples, beets or carrots, run the food through using the open blank first. Then, juice that "mush" through the machine a second time using the fine screen. Fresh juice is always the best, but these juices can be stored in the refrigerator in closed glass containers and enjoyed for up to two days. When I recommend serving juices in a fancy glass, use your best glasses and let it be a celebration. So, a toast to your health and enjoy your juicing results.

These tips should help you avoid any difficulties when using the Green Power machine:
• Go slowly.
• Put one piece of food in the feeding chute at a time.
• When you juice greens, have the gears clear of other food. The gears will pull in the greens (stalk side down) effortlessly.
• The machine is a bit fussy about apples and other soft fruit. Hard, firm, crisp fruit and vegetables juice best.
• When you are juicing a variety of foods, end with the firmest one. Carrots are generally best to end with when you are juicing vegetables. This technique ensures the softer foods get through the machine.
• If the machine starts to foam, stop putting food in and wait, letting the gears clear themselves.
• Loosening the outlet adjusting knob helps the pulp come out and avoids a back-up of food in the gears.
• With apples or pineapple, you may have to stop the machine, rinse it and reassemble it without the outlet adjusting knob. (Without the knob, the pulp is moister.)
• When juicing carrots, cut them the size of the feeding chute opening. Stand the carrot on end and trim off the parts needed to allow it to fit.

Baja Pineapple Drink

The cilantro and green lettuce in this recipe cut the sweetness of the pineapple. The mix also has a delightful taste. The ingredients also help prevent the sugar highs or lows some people experience from drinking plain pineapple juice.

1/2 pineapple
1/2 cup cilantro
3 greenleaf lettuce leaves
1 lime

Machine Instructions
Put the fine screen over the twin gears. Then attach the pulp discharge casing with the outlet adjusting knob in place, loosening the knob as you juice to allow the pulp to come out. Place the pitcher under the juice outlet to catch the juice, and a bowl under the pulp discharge outlet to catch the pulp.

Preparation and Serving Instructions
1. Shave off the prickly part of the pineapple skin. Cut pineapple across, not lengthwise, and into rectangular pieces.
2. Slice half a lime and juice the lime with its rind.
3. Juice pineapple, cilantro, lettuce leaves and the other half of the lime together.
4. Serve in a fancy glass, running lime around the rim of the glass. Garnish with lime and cilantro.

Preparation time: 10 minutes
Yields: 2 servings

Preparation Hints
Cutting the pineapple across in rings makes juicing the pineapple an easier task. There is more pulp in the juice if you slice the pineapple lengthwise. Also, when juicing any greens I make sure the machine is clear of food so the greens are then pulled directly into the gears, making the juicing effort minimal.

Ingredient Information
Pineapple has a special digestive enzyme, bromelain, which is helpful in reducing swelling in the body from an injury or bruise. Also, it can be helpful in reducing lung irritation from asthma. Vitamin A and chlorophyll from both the cilantro and lettuce are excellent for nourishing the hair and skin.

Berry Red Juice

This cooling juice is tops for cleaning blood and skin, and is a gentle nerve food, complete with a natural painkiller. This is a refreshing summer drink as melons are 92% water.

1/4 watermelon

1/2 cantaloupe

6 – 12 strawberries

Machine Instructions

Put the fine screen over the twin gears. Then attach the pulp discharge casing with the outlet adjusting knob in place, loosening the knob as you juice to allow the pulp to come out. Place the pitcher under the juice outlet to catch the juice, and a bowl under the pulp discharge outlet to catch the pulp.

Preparation and Serving Instructions

1. Juice the strawberries with the melon, including the rind and watermelon seeds.
2. Serve in a fancy glass garnished with a strawberry.

Preparation time: 10 minutes
Yields: 2 servings

Preparation Hints

If you want to make this a sweeter juice, do not include the rinds. If you want more calcium or protein, then include the rinds which are rich in chlorophyll and other minerals.

Ingredient Information

Melons are a natural diuretic and top-notch kidney and bladder cleansers. Rich in vitamin A and potassium, the melon juices have a toning effect on digestion. Strawberries, in addition to being a mild diuretic, also have a natural salicylate or organic painkiller, perfect for flushing out those aches and pains from overexertion.

Blushing Green Power Drink

Combining carrots with beets makes this juice a dynamite blood cleanser and liver tonic. The greens make this a perfect blend for the heart and lungs. It is an all-round body- building drink blushing with beet juice and powered by greens.

4 – 6 carrots
2 romaine lettuce leaves
1 beet
2 celery stalks
1/4 cup cilantro

Machine Instructions

Put the fine screen over the twin gears. Then attach the pulp discharge casing with the outlet adjusting knob in place, loosening the knob as you juice to allow the pulp to come out. Place the pitcher under the juice outlet to catch the juice, and a bowl under the pulp discharge outlet to catch the pulp.

Preparation and Serving Instructions

1. Cut carrots and beet to fit into the machine and let feed into the machine, alternating with the romaine, celery and cilantro.
2. Serve in a fancy glass.

Preparation time: 10 minutes
Yields: 2 servings

Preparation Hints

Make sure to keep the gears clear of food when juicing the greens.

Ingredient Information

Romaine is considered the "King of Lettuce" and carrots are the "King of Vegetables." What a royal combination for helping you create healthier blood. Beets are one of the best liver cleansers known, but be careful not to use too many beets in any juice. Cleansing is best done gradually. Celery helps to curb cravings for sweets, as it calms the nervous system with its concentration of organic alkaline minerals, especially sodium.

Bright Beet-Apple Surprise

One of my students, Wally Straton, suggested these ingredients. The lemon sparks the apple's flavor, but the beet gets us all blushing.

2 apples

1/4 beet

1/2 lemon

Machine Instructions

Put the fine screen over the twin gears. Then attach the pulp discharge casing with the outlet adjusting knob in place, loosening the knob as you juice to allow the pulp to come out. Place the pitcher under the juice outlet to catch the juice, and a bowl under the pulp discharge outlet to catch the pulp.

Preparation and Serving Instructions

1. Cut apples and beet into pieces, and juice together with 1/4 lemon with its rind.
2. Serve in fancy glass. Run a lemon around the rim of the glass and garnish with the wedge.

Preparation time: 10 minutes

Yields: 2 servings

Preparation Hints

Crisp apples, like Fujis, work best for this recipe. When juicing the apples, go slowly and put the skin side down first. Unscrew the outlet adjusting knob as needed to allow the pulp to be expelled.

Ingredient Information

This bright red juice treat has many benefits. Beet juice is one of the most valuable juices for helping to build up red corpuscles in the blood, while helping to cleanse the liver. Also, lemon juice stimulates the liver to make enzymes. A two-for-one special.

Gourmet Gerson Carrot-Apple Juice

1 apple

5 – 6 carrots

Machine Instructions

Put the open blank over the twin gears. Then attach the pulp discharge casing with the outlet adjusting knob in place. Place a bowl under both the juice outlet and the pulp discharge outlet to catch the food. Then, spoon the mixture into the juicer again. Use the fine screen instead of the open blank and repeat. Place a pitcher under the juice outlet to catch the juice and a bowl under the pulp discharge outlet to catch the pulp.

Preparation and Serving Instructions

1. Cut the apples and carrots into pieces that fit into the machine. Process or homogenize ingredients together.

Put the fine screen in place and spoon the food into the machine again—for juice.
2. Serve in a glass.

Preparation time: 10 minutes
Yields: 1 serving

Preparation Hints

Putting the food through a second time produces juice that stays fresh longer.

Ingredient Information

Dr. Max Gerson found that the pressed malic acid, from apples, enhances mineral absorption. Both apples and carrots help regulate digestion and elimination, and help reduce cholesterol.

C-Boost Drink

This recipe gets its name from the high vitamin C content in both apples and red bell peppers.

3 apples

3 celery stalks

1 red bell pepper

Machine Instructions

Put the fine screen over the twin gears. Then attach the pulp discharge casing with the outlet adjusting knob in place, loosening the knob as you juice to allow the pulp to come out. Place the pitcher under the juice outlet to catch the juice, and a bowl under the pulp discharge outlet to catch the pulp.

Preparation and Serving Instructions

1. Cut apples and bell pepper to fit into the machine, juicing only two of the celery stalks with the rest of the ingredients.
2. Serve in a fancy glass, with a celery stalk as a stirrer.

Preparation time: 10 minutes
Yields: 2 servings

Preparation Hints

Long strips of the bell pepper fit best into the machine. Using celery stalks that have leaves on the top makes a bright and lovely stirrer.

Ingredient Information

Red bell peppers are actually ripe green bell peppers. Once ripe, bell peppers are one of the richest sources of vitamin C. Apples are also rich in pepsin, a naturally occurring digestive enzyme. The celery, known for its high sodium content, helps balance the functioning of our hearts. Fuji apples are especially flavorful. Find your favorites amongst the varieties that grow in your area. It is best to store apples in a cool place.

Coffee Quitter's Juice

One of my students came to class so excited because he had been able to give up coffee. We asked him how, and he said he made this juice and he felt so good, he did not need to drink coffee. If you are ready to kick the habit, here is his recipe.

1 pear

2 apples

4 oranges

1 grapefruit

Machine Instructions

Put the fine screen over the twin gears. Then attach the pulp discharge casing with the outlet adjusting knob in place, loosening the knob as you juice to allow the pulp to come out. Place the pitcher under the juice outlet to catch the juice, and a bowl under the pulp discharge outlet to catch the pulp.

Preparation and Serving Instructions

1. Peel and cut the oranges and grapefruit, and cut the apples and pear to fit into the machine. Juice all the ingredients.
2. Serve in a fancy glass.

Preparation time: 10 minutes
Yields: 4 servings

Preparation Hints

Keep the white part of the orange and grapefruit on the fruit for a creamier juice, rich in bioflavonoids.

Ingredient Information

The brain needs a powerful substitute to let go of such an addictive drug as caffeine. This combination of vitamin and mineral-rich juices will do what is needed for you to become caffeine-free.

Digester's Delight Juice

The celery is the surprise ingredient in this delightful drink. It can make this a salty drink, so go lightly with it at first, adding more to taste.

1 pineapple, skinned
3 – 4 oranges (peeled)
3 celery stalks (juice one stalk to start with)
2 apples

Machine Instructions
Put the fine screen over the twin gears. Then attach the pulp discharge casing with the outlet adjusting knob in place, loosening the knob as you juice to allow the pulp to come out. Place the pitcher under the juice outlet to catch the juice, and a bowl under the pulp discharge outlet to catch the pulp.

Preparation and Serving Instructions
1. Peel and cut pineapple in rings and then slices. Put through the machine with the peeled oranges and apple, alternating with one of the celery stalks.
2. Serve with a celery stick stirrer in a fancy glass.

Preparation time: 15 minutes
Yields: 4 servings

Preparation Hints
It is best to juice firm pineapples. Occasionally, if a mushy pineapple is juiced, the screen will get clogged. Just stop the machine, rinse off the screen and then carry on juicing.

Ingredient Information
Oranges are high in vitamin C and calcium. I used to think that an orange had to be the color orange to be ripe, but not so. Most oranges are gassed with ethylene or colored with red dye to render the fruit a cosmetic orange color. Oranges, in fact, can be eaten slightly green. Remember, the white part next to the skin has the bioflavonoids which greatly enhance the body's absorption of vitamin C. So, juice it, do not peel it off.

"How Do You Spell Relief ?" Juice

Relief is spelled: j-u-i-c-e.
This juice's rich digestive aids from both the apple and cabbage give new meaning to the word relief.

1 apple
6 carrots
2 slices of purple cabbage

Machine Instructions
Put the fine screen over the twin gears. Attach the pulp discharge casing with the outlet adjusting knob in place, loosening the knob as you juice to allow the pulp to come out. Place the pitcher under the juice outlet to catch the juice, and a bowl under the pulp discharge outlet to catch the pulp.

Preparation and Serving Instructions
1. Cut the apple, carrot and cabbage in the appropriate sizes and alternate putting the different ingredients into the machine. Juice all ingredients.
2. Serve in a fancy glass.

Preparation time: 10 minutes
Yields: 2 servings

Preparation Hints
End juicing with carrots to help push all the ingredients through the machine.

Ingredient Information
Every juicing book I have read sings the praises of this combination of produce. For those who have problems with digesting cabbage juice, the apple blends and smoothes out the difficulties. The pepsin in the apples is a useful digestive aid.

How Sweet Anise Is Drink

Carrot and celery juices combined are an electrolyte balancer in hot weather. Our bodies lose sodium in hot weather, and this juice replenishes and rejuvenates us.

8 carrots
2 fresh anise stalks
3 – 4 celery stalks
2 apples

Machine Instructions
Put the fine screen over the twin gears. Then attach the pulp discharge casing with the outlet adjusting knob in place, loosening the knob as you juice to allow the pulp to come out. Place the pitcher under the juice outlet to catch the juice, and a bowl under the pulp discharge outlet to catch the pulp.

Preparation and Serving Instructions
1. Cut the carrots, anise and apples to fit and let feed into the machine. Juice all ingredients.
2. Serve in a fancy glass.

Preparation time: 10 minutes
Yields: 2 servings

Preparation Hints
The tops of the anise can be juiced as well as the white part on the bottom.

Ingredient Information
There is a popular misconception that carrot juice causes the skin to turn orange. That is not the reason the skin may discolor. As in any colorful juice, the coloring does not come through to the skin's surface. In fact, if your skin does discolor it is because the liver is cleansing and some of the color from the toxins is being eliminated from the liver.

Fat Melt Down Juice

This juice helps reduce fat from the places we tend to store cellulite—arms and lower body. Plus, the ginger warms and stimulates the blood to circulate while we are slimming down.

2 apples
2 pears
1 slice of fresh ginger

Machine Instructions
Put the fine screen over the twin gears. Then attach the pulp discharge casing without the outlet adjusting knob. Place the pitcher under the juice outlet to catch the juice, and a bowl under the pulp discharge outlet to catch the pulp.

Preparation and Serving Instructions
1. Cut apples and pears to fit into the machine. Juice all ingredients alternating with sliced apples, pears and ginger.
2. Serve in a fancy glass.

Preparation time: 10 minutes
Yields: 2 servings

Preparation Hints
Remove the hard stems first. The rest of the apple and pear can be juiced, peeling only if the skin is waxed. Mealy apples make better sauce than juice, so only use crisp, hard apples and firm pears for juicing. Juice slowly, putting the fruit in skin side down. Because of the slowness of the trituration process, if you try to juice soft apples or juice too quickly you will make apple-pear sauce and not juice. The fresh ginger can be used with the skin intact. Ginger has a strong flavor, a little goes a long way, so use gingerly.

Ingredient Information
Fuji, Golden Delicious, Gala, Granny Smith, Macintosh and Pippin are among the many varieties that can be chosen for juicing. The high pectin content from the apple juice forms a gel in our intestines. This gel absorbs and dissolves toxins and stimulates the bowel, regulating elimination. Anjou, Bartlett or Bosc pears are wonderful for juicing. Along with having vitamins A, B_1, B_2, C, folic acid and niacin, pears are also rich in many minerals, supplying phosphorous, potassium, chlorine, iron, magnesium, sodium, sulfur and a little calcium. Go easy on this juice because pear juice does have diuretic and laxative effects.

Bunnies Will Stay Juice

If I was a bunny I would stick around to enjoy this juice. This blend of ingredients will bring out the spring in your step and the hop in your hike.

4 – 6 carrots

1 kale leaf

1 cucumber

1 apple

1/4 cup parsley

1 anise stalk

Machine Instructions

Put the fine screen over the twin gears. Then attach the pulp discharge casing with the outlet adjusting knob in place, loosening the knob as you juice to allow the pulp to come out. Place the pitcher under the juice outlet to catch the juice, and a bowl under the pulp discharge outlet to catch the pulp.

Preparation and Serving Instructions

1. Cut ingredients to fit into the machine and let feed, alternating ingredients.
2. Serve in a fancy glass.

Preparation time: 10 minutes
Yields: 2 servings

Preparation Hints

Slicing the cucumber lengthwise makes juicing easier. Make sure to find unwaxed cucumbers or peel off the waxed skin.

Ingredient Information

The high potassium content of the cucumber makes this juice valuable in reducing high and low blood pressure as well as gum and teeth afflictions. Cucumber's high silicon content makes this juice beneficial against nail splitting and hair loss. Anise has such a delightful licorice taste and helps digestion.

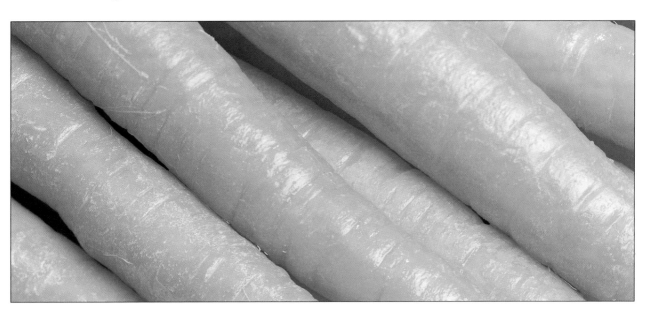

Garden Delight Juice

This bright beet juice is both refreshing and cooling. A delight on a warm afternoon or as an evening cocktail.

4 – 6 carrots
1 beet
2 celery stalks
1 small cucumber unwaxed

Machine Instructions

Put the fine screen over the twin gears. Then attach the pulp discharge casing with the outlet adjusting knob in place, loosening the knob as you juice to allow the pulp to come out. Place the pitcher under the juice outlet to catch the juice, and a bowl under the pulp discharge outlet to catch the pulp.

Preparation and Serving Instructions

1. Cut carrots, beet and cucumber to fit into the machine. Juice together, alternating ingredients.
2. Serve in a fancy glass.

Preparation time: 10 minutes
Yields: 2 servings

Preparation Hints

When juicing an extra large carrot, hold the carrot upright, and slice down around the thickest part, shrinking its diameter. Lying it down on the cutting board can be awkward. On the other hand, cutting a cucumber on its side is easier.

Ingredient Information

Whether you are calming your nerves with celery's high sodium content or feeding your hair and nails with the cucumber's high silicon and sulfur content, this juice helps bring the garden's finest together. The alkaline minerals, especially the magnesium and calcium from the carrots help to strengthen the bones and teeth. Beets, with their abundance of alkaline minerals such as potassium and calcium, help to cleanse and build the blood. What gifts the garden offers us.

Green Powered Juice

This is a four star juice. All the ingredients are exceptional foods for cleaning the blood and strengthening the liver. The ginger is good for warming up the body on a cold day. Even used alone, each of these ingredients does wonders for our health.

4 handfuls of wheatgrass
2 apples
4 – 6 carrots
1 thin slice fresh ginger

Machine Instructions

Put the fine screen over the twin gears. Then attach the pulp discharge casing with the outlet adjusting knob in place, loosening the knob as you juice to allow the pulp to come out. Place the pitcher under the juice outlet to catch the juice, and a bowl under the pulp discharge outlet to catch the pulp.

Preparation and Serving Instructions

1. Cut wheatgrass and let feed into the machine, alternating with sliced apples, carrots and ginger. Juice all ingredients.
2. Serve in a fancy glass.

Preparation time: 10 minutes
Yields: 2 servings

Preparation Hints

Using firm apples will help speed up the juicing process because the gears will be able to grasp the chunks and pull them into the machine.

Ingredient Information

Wheatgrass is a terrific blood cleanser, plus it provides us with our daily requirement of chlorophyll. Wheatgrass combined with apple and carrot juice offers the body vitamin C, beta carotene and a host of other vitamins to help cleanse and rebuild the blood.

Green Green Juice

This juice is loaded with chlorophyll. Go easy on the kale, unless you like its flavor. Celery will make the juice more salty. Anise will sweeten with a licorice flavor. Cucumber and romaine are mellow flavors and apple is sweet. Try "chewing" the juice in your mouth to experience the flavors.

1 kale leaf
2 celery stalks
2 apples
1 medium cucumber, unwaxed
2 romaine leaves
1 – 2 anise stalks
(the white and the green stalk part)

Machine Instructions
Put the fine screen over the twin gears. Then attach the pulp discharge casing with the outlet adjusting knob in place, loosening the knob as you juice to allow the pulp to come out. Place the pitcher under the juice outlet to catch the juice, and a bowl under the pulp discharge outlet to catch the pulp.

Preparation and Serving Instructions
1. Cut the apples and cucumber to fit into the machine. Juice it all together, alternating ingredients.
2. Serve in a fancy glass, using an anise stalk as a stirrer for each glass.

Preparation time: 10 minutes
Yields: 2 servings

Preparation Hints
Keep the gears clear so the greens can be pulled through. Keep the outlet adjusting knob loose.

Ingredient Information
Chlorophyll is the best substance for helping to balance our system. This juice is rich in chlorophyll from many sources - the kale, romaine and cucumber skin. The apple and anise help digestion, celery calms the nerves, and cucumber is good for our hair and nails. If you like the taste of green and sweet, you will love this juice.

Orange Orange Juice

While most juices can be stored, this one is special. It needs to be used as it is juiced. If you store it, this juice will get bitter. So, enjoy this one fresh from the machine.

6 carrots
4 oranges

Machine Instructions
Put the fine screen over the twin gears. Then attach the pulp discharge casing with the outlet adjusting knob in place, loosening the knob as you juice to allow the pulp to come out. Place the pitcher under the juice outlet to catch the juice, and a bowl under the pulp discharge outlet to catch the pulp.

Preparation and Serving Instructions
1. Peel and cut the oranges and carrots into pieces that fit and let feed into the machine. Juice all ingredients.
2. Serve in a fancy glass.

Preparation time: 10 minutes
Yields: 2 servings

Preparation Hints
Alternating the oranges with the carrots helps the juicer work at its best.

Ingredient Information
Oranges and carrots are both high in calcium. Plus, the orange juice cleanses and helps to tone the intestinal tract. Contrary to popular opinion, overly acidic blood is alkalized by drinking orange juice on a regular basis. Drink two to three 6 ounce glasses per week of fresh orange juice, not the commercial variety.

Falling into Winter

Eating with the seasons helps keep our bodies in balance. The ingredients in this juice are typically fall or winter fare. Find your favorites to juice. We had a garden in Arizona and could choose from three types of kale, curly leafed, purple, or the dark green. Most people can find these varieties in farmers' markets.

4 – 6 carrots
1 kale leaf
1 celery stalk
1 apple

Machine Instructions
Put the fine screen over the twin gears. Then attach the pulp discharge casing with the outlet adjusting knob in place, loosening the knob as you juice to allow the pulp to come out. Place the pitcher under the juice outlet to catch the juice, and a bowl under the pulp discharge outlet to catch the pulp.

Preparation and Serving Instructions
1. Cut carrots and apple to fit into the machine and juice, alternating the ingredients.
2. Serve in a fancy glass.

Preparation time: 10 minutes
Yields: 2 servings

Preparation Hints
The kale and celery feed best by putting the stalk end in first, with the gears clear of other ingredients.

Ingredient Information
Carrot juice is one of the best balancers of our entire system. It is a rich source of pro-vitamin A, and it contains vitamins B, C, D, E, G and K. Rich in beta-carotene, it is a natural solvent for ulcerous and cancerous conditions. In combination with kale (part of the cabbage family), the vitamin C content in carrots is enhanced, making this drink particularly beneficial for ulcerous conditions and gum infections.

Finaisely Juiced Delight

The contrast of the sweet pineapple and the salty celery, tweaked by the unexpected licorice flavor of the anise makes this drink a pleasant surprise.

1 pineapple
2 anise stalks with top greens
3 celery stalks

Machine Instructions
Put the fine screen over the twin gears. Then attach the pulp discharge casing without the outlet adjusting knob. Place the pitcher under the juice outlet to catch the juice, and a bowl under the pulp discharge outlet to catch the pulp.

Preparation and Serving Instructions
1. Cut skinned pineapple in rings and then slices, juicing with the anise and two celery stalks, alternating the ingredients.
2. Serve with a celery stick stirrer in a fancy glass.

Preparation time: 15 minutes
Yields: 4 servings

Preparation Hints
As with any pineapple juice, use only firm, golden skin-colored pineapples. When juicing the anise or celery, make sure the chute is empty of all other food. This way the gears will pull the crunchy stalks through effortlessly.

Ingredient Information
Anise soothes sore throats, assists digestion and cleanses the palate. Added to bromelain's (from the pineapple) ability to balance fluids that are too acidic or too alkaline and to stimulate hormonal secretions in the pancreas, this juice is a thirst quenching dream. Also, your nervous system can be calmed by the celery juice, due to its high concentration of organic alkaline minerals, especially sodium.

If We Cantaloupe Juice

Picking out a ripe cantaloupe is half the fun. If it smells sweet where the stem would be (the soft spot on top), feels reasonably firm and is evenly round, it is probably a tasty cantaloupe.

1/4 watermelon

1/2 cantaloupe

Machine Instructions
Put the fine screen over the twin gears. Then attach the pulp discharge casing with the outlet adjusting knob in place, loosening the knob as you juice to allow the pulp to come out. Place the pitcher under the juice outlet to catch the juice, and a bowl under the pulp discharge outlet to catch the pulp.

Preparation and Serving Instructions
1. Cut watermelon and cantaloupe into pieces that fit and let feed into the machine. Juice all ingredients.

2. Serve in a fancy glass.

Preparation time: 10 minutes
Yields: 2 servings

Preparation Hints
If you want a sweeter juice, do not include the watermelon rind or cantaloupe rind. Otherwise, include the rind as it has valuable nutrients such as calcium.

Ingredient Information
Cantaloupe has a remarkably high vitamin A and C content.

Ummm Cocktail

There are two choices of grapefruit for you to choose from, white and pink.
Which one do you prefer?

1 grapefruit

3 apples

1 celery stalk

Machine Instructions

Put the fine screen over the twin gears. Then attach the pulp discharge casing with the outlet adjusting knob in place, loosening the knob as you juice to allow the pulp to come out. Place the pitcher under the juice outlet to catch the juice, and a bowl under the pulp discharge outlet to catch the pulp.

Preparation and Serving Instructions

1. Peel and cut the grapefruit, and cut the apples into pieces that fit and let feed into the machine. Juice all ingredients.
2. Serve in a fancy glass.

Preparation time: 10 minutes
Yields: 2 servings

Preparation Hints

Leave some of the white part of the grapefruit intact, and juice. It will make the juice creamy and rich in nutrients. Here again, the outlet adjusting knob might need to be taken off entirely to create a foamless juice.

Ingredient Information

The ruby or pink grapefruit is mainly grown in Texas. They are sweeter and generally less acidic than the white ones. The white part next to the fruit is rich in bioflavonoids, which help the body utilize vitamin C. This combination helps to strengthen our capillary walls. However, citrus taken in excess can actually leech calcium from the system. Find the balance for your system. Rotating your food, eating or drinking it only every three or four days can help avoid overdoing any one ingredient.

Juicing Up

The unique ingredient in this drink is the spice, either basil or parsley, juiced with the citrus and apple. Try them both, one at a time, and see what you prefer. These spices add chlorophyll, which helps to balance the sugar from the fruits.

1 grapefruit
1 apple
3 tangerines
pinch of basil or parsley

Machine Instructions
Put the fine screen over the twin gears. Then attach the pulp discharge casing with the outlet adjusting knob in place, loosening the knob as you juice to allow the pulp to come out. Place the pitcher under the juice outlet to catch the juice, and a bowl under the pulp discharge outlet to catch the pulp.

Preparation and Serving Instructions
1. Peel the grapefruit and tangerines and cut into pieces that fit into the machine. Juice all ingredients.
2. Serve in a fancy glass.

Preparation time: 10 minutes
Yields: 2 servings

Preparation Hints
This juice may not need the outlet adjusting knob tightly in place because the gears need to be loose to pull in the thick chunks of food. Put it on loosely and see if it is needed. If any foaming happens, remove the knob.

Menopause Tonic

Women going through menopause will be pleased to get their hands on this energizing and balancing recipe.

6 carrots
1 beet
6 – 8 spinach leaves
2 celery stalks

Machine Instructions
Put the fine screen over the twin gears. Then attach the pulp discharge casing with the outlet adjusting knob in place, loosening the knob as you juice to allow the pulp to come out. Place the pitcher under the juice outlet to catch the juice, and a bowl under the pulp discharge outlet to catch the pulp.

Preparation and Serving Instructions
1. Cut carrots into pieces that fit and let feed into the machine. Juice all ingredients.
2. Serve in a fancy glass.

Preparation time: 10 minutes
Yields: 2 servings

Preparation Hints
Let the spinach get pulled into the gears on their own. Just clear out any other food, and let the machine do its thing.

Ingredient Information
The carrots, beets and spinach all help to cleanse the liver. The celery helps to calm the nerves with its high concentration of sodium. Also, celery helps to reduce cravings for sweets.

Lean Green Pineapple Juice Treat

This drink shows what happens when a fruit high in vitamins A, B-complex and C mixes with greens high in calcium, magnesium and iron—magic. The greens mellow the taste of the pineapple and make the fruit sugar more easily assimilated.

1/2 pineapple
1/4 cup fresh parsley
3 romaine leaves

Machine Instructions
Put the fine screen over the twin gears. Then attach the pulp discharge casing with the outlet adjusting knob in place, loosening the knob as you juice to allow the pulp to come out. Place the pitcher under the juice outlet to catch the juice, and a bowl under the pulp discharge outlet to catch the pulp.

Preparation and Serving Instructions
1. Cut the skin off the pineapple and into pieces that fit and let feed into the machine. Juice all ingredients, ending with the pineapple.
2. Serve in a fancy glass.

Preparation time: 10 minutes
Yields: 2 servings

Preparation Hints
The greens juice easier with the stem, or narrow end, down and the gears clear of any other food.

Ingredient Information
To pick a ripe pineapple, pull out one of the leaves on the top. If it pulls out easily, and the bottom end smells sweet, you have found a ripe one. Romaine's rich sodium content, 60% higher than its potassium content, makes this one of the most beneficial juices for regulating the adrenal glands.

Pineapple "Celapple" Cocktail

Some folks feel it is not proper food combining to mix fruits with vegetables. This juice is an exception to that rule. Juicing fruits and vegetables allows for more successful digestion of the two because the bulky fiber is removed.

1/2 pineapple
1 – 2 apples
2 – 3 celery stalks

Machine Instructions
Put the fine screen over the twin gears. Then attach the pulp discharge casing with the outlet adjusting knob in place, loosening the knob as you juice to allow the pulp to come out. Place the pitcher under the juice outlet to catch the juice, and a bowl under the pulp discharge outlet to catch the pulp.

Preparation and Serving Instructions
1. Peel and cut the pineapple, and cut but do not peel the apples into pieces that fit. Feed all ingredients into the machine.
2. Serve in a fancy glass.

Preparation time: 10 minutes
Yields: 2 servings
Preparation Hints
Cutting the pineapple into slices and then into wedges that fit into the machine makes for less foam in the juice. If there is too much foam, remove the outlet adjusting knob.

Ingredient Information
People with arthritis often complain that they cannot drink pineapple juice. The irony of that statement is that the bromelain, the active enzyme in pineapple is an effective natural anti-inflammatory agent which helps arthritis. This information was published in the *Journal of Ethnopharmacology* in 1988, vol. 22. Over 200 scientific papers document the efficacy of bromelain in reducing inflammation.

Orange You Glad It's Lemonade

This juice is one my summer favorites. This combination of ingredients tastes remarkably fresh, and is sweet without adding any refined sugar.

2 apples

2 oranges

1/4 lemon

Machine Instructions

Put the fine screen over the twin gears. Then attach the pulp discharge casing with the outlet adjusting knob in place, loosening the knob as you juice to allow the pulp to come out. Place the pitcher under the juice outlet to catch the juice, and a bowl under the pulp discharge outlet to catch the pulp.

Preparation and Serving Instructions

1. Juice together peeled oranges, sliced apples and lemon with its rind.
2. Serve in a fancy glass, garnished with a lemon wedge.

Preparation time: 10 minutes
Yields: 2 servings

Preparation Hints

For a taste treat, run part of the lemon around the rim of the glass. What a delightful flavor burst when you taste the zingy lemon then the sweet juice!

Ingredient Information

Apple juice is a bowel regulator due to its pectin and malic acid content. Apples and oranges are rich in many of the same vitamins A, B1, B2, B6, and C, biotin, folic acid and a host of minerals. This drink is your multi-vitamin for the day.

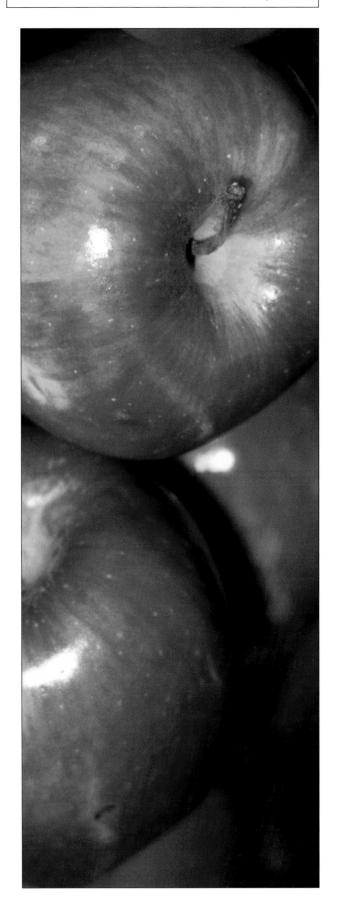

Que Bueno Juice

Literally translated this means, "what a good juice." Jicama is a water-rich food, sweet like a white carrot. On a hot day in Mexico you can find street vendors on the street selling jicama with salt and lime juice as a snack.

8 carrots
1/2 jicama (peeled)
3 celery stalks
1 lime

Machine Instructions
Put the fine screen over the twin gears. Then attach the pulp discharge casing with the outlet adjusting knob in place, loosening the knob as you juice to allow the pulp to come out. Place the pitcher under the juice outlet to catch the juice, and a bowl under the pulp discharge outlet to catch the pulp.

Preparation and Serving Instructions
1. Cut carrots and jicama into pieces that fit and let feed into the machine. Juice all ingredients except the lime. Hand squeeze the lime juice into each glass.
2. Serve in a fancy glass.

Preparation time: 10 minutes
Yields: 2 servings

Preparation Hints
For a tangy taste, run a lime wedge around the rim of the glass.

Ingredient Information
Lime juice is similar to lemon, only it is not as acidic, and therefore not as strong a cleanser. Believe it or not, limes are ripe when they are yellow. The green ones in the supermarkets have been picked too early.

Orient Express Juice

One way to build strong bones is with plenty of dark green leafy vegetables. The calcium and magnesium in the bok choy, carrots and napa cabbage are yours to assimilate.

2 bok choy stalks
6 carrots
2 napa cabbage leaves
1 apple

Machine Instructions
Put the fine screen over the twin gears. Then attach the pulp discharge casing with the outlet adjusting knob in place, loosening the knob as you juice to allow the pulp to come out. Place the pitcher under the juice outlet to catch the juice, and a bowl under the pulp discharge outlet to catch the pulp.

Preparation and Serving Instructions
1. Cut carrots, greens and apples into pieces that fit and let feed into the machine. Juice all ingredients.
2. Serve in a fancy glass.

Preparation time: 10 minutes
Yields: 2 servings

Preparation Hints
Put the bok choy and cabbage stalk bottoms down for easy juicing.

Ingredient Information
The Greeks considered cabbage to be a tonic and rejuvenator, as well as a "cure" for baldness. Though it may not cure baldness, it is an effective laxative and healing agent for skin complaints and intestinal ulcers. Vitamin U is believed to be the active ingredient in cabbage juice that helps to heal ulcers.

Blood Tonic

The foundation of our health is based on the quality of our blood. This drink has all the best blood builders and cleansers - a true tonic.

1 cup wheatgrass
4 – 6 carrots
1 beet
1/2 cup Italian parsley
2 celery stalks

Machine Instructions
Put the fine screen over the twin gears. Then attach the pulp discharge casing with the outlet adjusting knob in place, loosening the knob as you juice to allow the pulp to come out. Place the pitcher under the juice outlet to catch the juice, and a bowl under the pulp discharge outlet to catch the pulp.

Preparation and Serving Instructions
1. Cut wheatgrass and let feed into the machine, alternating with parsley, celery and sliced carrots and beets. Juice all ingredients.
2. Serve in a fancy glass.

Preparation time: 10 minutes
Yields: 2 servings

Preparation Hints
Any juice with greens does better when there is open access to the twin gears. This machine does not like being overloaded with ingredients. Sometimes greens clump together after being juiced. If this happens, a bit of stirring with a spoon or shaking in a sealed container smoothes out the clumps.

Ingredient Information
Wheatgrass is one of the best blood cleansers. It is high in chlorophyll, a molecule that closely resembles hemoglobin found in the red blood cells. Parsley, also full of chlorophyll, stimulates oxygen metabolism, as well as cell respiration and regeneration. Parsley, combined with the pro-vitamin A-rich carrots, sodium-rich celery and alkaline mineral-rich beets, aid in building the red blood cell count. Who could ask for a better blood tonic?

Pulsating Parsley Juice

Your pulse will beat more easily with this drink in your system. Also, these blood cleansers will also help you rebuild your blood.

6 carrots

1 beet

8 spinach leaves

1/4 cup fresh parsley

Machine Instructions

Put the fine screen over the twin gears. Then attach the pulp discharge casing with the outlet adjusting knob in place, loosening the knob as you juice to allow the pulp to come out. Place the pitcher under the juice outlet to catch the juice, and a bowl under the pulp discharge outlet to catch the pulp.

Preparation and Serving Instructions

1. Cut carrots and beet into pieces that fit and let feed into the machine. Juice all ingredients.
2. Serve in a fancy glass.

Preparation time: 10 minutes
Yields: 2 servings

Preparation Hints

Put the spinach and parsley stalk down for easy juicing.

Ingredient Information

Spinach juice, because of its high concentration of alkaline minerals, is especially strengthening to the teeth and gums. But, because of its high oxalic acid content, it should be used moderately. In short, do not drink a lot of spinach juice or you will be exercising all day to metabolize the oxalic acid.

Tropical Juice Blend

One of the beauties of the Green Power machine is that it can juice such a wide variety of foods, from wheatgrass to pineapple. This juice has a delightful blend of both and is sweet, green and salty.

1 handful of wheatgrass

1/2 pineapple

2 celery stalks

Machine Instructions

Put the fine screen over the twin gears. Then attach the pulp discharge casing with the outlet adjusting knob in place, loosening the knob as you juice to allow the pulp to come out. Place the pitcher under the juice outlet to catch the juice, and a bowl under the pulp discharge outlet to catch the pulp.

Preparation and Serving Instructions

1. Peel and cut the pineapple into pieces that fit and let feed into the machine. Juice all ingredients.
2. Serve in a fancy glass.

Preparation time: 10 minutes
Yields: 2 servings

Preparation Hints

The wheatgrass will be pulled right through the machine on its own if the gears are clear. Slicing the pineapple in rings and then wedges is the easiest way to prepare a foamless juice.

Ingredient Information

Wheatgrass juice has many anti-aging properties including vitamins A, B-complex, C and E, chlorophyll, super oxide dismutase and a full spectrum of minerals and trace elements. It benefits the blood cells, bones, glands, the kidneys, liver, muscles, spleen and teeth - a regular full body workout.

Pineapple Juiced Delight

If you have any swelling, this juice can help reduce it. Mix up a drink for yourself and see if it works for you. But, you can enjoy this drink without needing to be injured.

1/2 pineapple
4 oranges
2 celery stalks

Machine Instructions
Put the fine screen over the twin gears. Then attach the pulp discharge casing with the outlet adjusting knob in place, loosening the knob as you juice to allow the pulp to come out. Place the pitcher under the juice outlet to catch the juice, and a bowl under the pulp discharge outlet to catch the pulp.

Preparation and Serving Instructions
1. Peel and cut the pineapple and oranges into pieces that fit and let feed into the machine. Juice all ingredients.
2. Serve in a fancy glass.

Preparation time: 10 minutes
Yields: 2 servings

Preparation Hints
The celery has a salty flavor, so use less if you find it too salty. Use more if you like the contrast of flavors.

Ingredient Information
Pineapple is actually native to South America. I always thought it was originally from Hawaii. It is not a fruit in the ordinary sense of the word because it forms when the fruits of a hundred or more separate flowers coalesce. It certainly is a rich and sweet fruit to enjoy, whether juiced or blended.

Wheatgrass Cocktail

The lemon juice makes this cocktail sparkle. Whenever I drink wheatgrass by itself, I usually like a carrot juice chaser. Well, this drink has the chaser in the glass.

1 handful of wheatgrass

8 carrots

1 lemon

Machine Instructions
Put the fine screen over the twin gears. Then attach the pulp discharge casing with the outlet adjusting knob in place, loosening the knob as you juice to allow the pulp to come out. Place the pitcher under the juice outlet to catch the juice, and a bowl under the pulp discharge outlet to catch the pulp.

Preparation and Serving Instructions
1. Cut carrots into pieces that fit and let feed into the machine. Juice all ingredients except the lemon. Hand squeeze a little lemon juice into each glass.
2. Serve in a fancy glass.

Preparation time: 10 minutes
Yields: 2 servings

Preparation Hints
Running a lemon wedge around the edge of the glass is a taste treat worth doing as is a squirt of lemon in the juice.

Ingredient Information
For those of us who live or visit polluted, smog-filled areas, wheatgrass juice protects the lungs and blood from some of that air and water pollution. For more information on this fascinating food, read Ann Wigmore's *The Wheatgrass Book*.

Sweet Liquid Treat

This delightfully sweet drink is enhanced by the anise which is part of the celery family and an efficient blood builder.

8 - 12 carrots
1/2 beet
2 anise stalks
1 cucumber, unwaxed

Machine Instructions
Put the fine screen over the twin gears. Then attach the pulp discharge casing with the outlet adjusting knob in place, loosening the knob as you juice to allow the pulp to come out. Place the pitcher under the juice outlet to catch the juice, and a bowl under the pulp discharge outlet to catch the pulp.

Preparation and Serving Instructions
1. Cut carrots, beet, anise and cucumber to fit. Juice all ingredients.
2. Serve in a fancy glass.

Preparation time: 10 minutes
Yields: 2 servings

Preparation Hints
Cucumbers can be found unwaxed even in regular supermarkets. Usually they are either the hot house or pickling variety. The skin of the cucumber has most of the vitamin A. If you can only find waxed cucumbers, peel off the wax as it does not juice well. Juicing cucumber without its peel with carrots makes up for some of the loss vitamin A.

Ingredient Information
Cucumber is a cooling vegetable. It actually helps the body cool down in hot weather. It is also a natural diuretic and helps to dissolve kidney stones. Its high potassium content promotes flexibility in the muscles, and is often called the "youth mineral." Cucumber is used by many salons as a skin and facial toner.

Sweet Popeye Blend

Popeye got his spinach from a can. This way is so much healthier — in a glass, freshly juiced.

1/2 cup fresh spinach
1/2 cup arugula
8 carrots
2 slices fresh anise

Machine Instructions
Put the fine screen over the twin gears. Then attach the pulp discharge casing with the outlet adjusting knob in place, loosening the knob as you juice to allow the pulp to come out. Place the pitcher under the juice outlet to catch the juice, and a bowl under the pulp discharge outlet to catch the pulp.

Preparation and Serving Instructions
1. Cut carrots and anise into pieces that fit and let feed into the machine. Juice all ingredients.
2. Serve in a fancy glass.

Preparation time: 10 minutes
Yields: 2 servings

Preparation Hints
When the gears are clear and unencumbered, the greens will easily slide through the machine.

Ingredient Information
Spinach is said to be one of the most beneficial foods for the entire digestive tract, both for the alimentary section (your stomach through to your small intestine) and the large intestine. Eaten raw, spinach is one of the best cleansing, reconstructive and regenerative foods for the intestinal tract. Also, it is very effective for helping the gums and teeth stay healthy. Arugula is stimulating for the liver and lungs. As with other dark green leafy members of the cabbage family, arugula is a rich source of calcium and is full of phytochemicals—recommended as a cancer preventative food by the American Cancer Society.

Yummy for the Tummy

We do so much to deplete our bodies' health, this puts some back by helping to rebuild our blood, digestion and health.

6 carrots
1 apple
2 celery stalks
1/4 cup fresh parsley

Machine Instructions

Put the fine screen over the twin gears. Then attach the pulp discharge casing with the outlet adjusting knob in place, loosening the knob as you juice to allow the pulp to come out. Place the pitcher under the juice outlet to catch the juice, and a bowl under the pulp discharge outlet to catch the pulp.

Preparation and Serving Instructions

1. Cut carrots and apples into pieces that fit and let feed into the machine. Juice all ingredients.
2. Serve in a fancy glass.

Preparation time: 10 minutes
Yields: 2 servings

Preparation Hints

Put the parsley in stem first. Occasionally, parsley juice gets a little clumpy. Just stir it in with the other juice and it will unclump.

Ingredient Information

Parsley is high in iron, another blood builder. Apples' high vitamin C content helps prevent colds, flu and intestinal infections. It helps the body's elaborate defense system fight against bacterial infections. Carrots build the blood, and celery calms the nervous system. With this juice, you are on the road to a brand new you.

Jae's Favorite

My good friend Jae Choi's favorite juice is a combination of three health-promoting fruits and vegetables - carrots, apples and celery. These ingredients all provide vital nutrients and their flavors combine well.

6 carrots
2 apples
2 celery stalks

Machine Instructions

Put the fine screen over the twin gears. Then attach the pulp discharge casing with the outlet adjusting knob in place, loosening the knob as you juice to allow the pulp to come out. Place the pitcher under the juice outlet to catch the juice, and a bowl under the pulp discharge outlet to catch the pulp.

Preparation and Serving Instructions

1. Cut the carrots and apples into pieces that fit and let feed into the machine.
   Juice all ingredients.
2. Serve in a fancy glass.

Preparation time: 10 minutes
Yields: 2 servings

Preparation Hints

Using firm apples is important. The outlet adjusting knob can be loosened quite a bit to avoid any foaming of the apple juice. End by juicing a carrot to get all the ingredients through the machine.

Ingredient Information

Jae has good sense picking this juice as his favorite because the ingredients are all beneficial for the digestive system. When food can be processed and eliminated with ease, it retains nutrients and expels toxins, promoting better functioning of other body systems.

Omega 3 Oils Blend

Our body needs essential fatty acids. Flax seeds provide us with these oils and is a wonderful brain food. This drink is as tasty as it is healthy.

4 oranges

2 grapefruit

1/2 cup fresh parsley, or cilantro

2 Tbsp flax seeds
(soak 2 - 4 hours, no rinsing necessary)

Machine Instructions

Put the fine screen over the twin gears. Then attach the pulp discharge casing with the outlet adjusting knob in place, loosening the knob as you juice to allow the pulp to come out. Place the pitcher under the outlet to catch the juice, and a bowl under the discharge outlet to catch the pulp.

Preparation and Serving Instructions

1. Peel and cut the oranges and grapefruit into pieces that fit into the machine and juice.
2. In a blender, mix the soaked flax seeds, parsley or cilantro with the juice.
3. Serve in a fancy glass, garnished with parsley or cilantro.

Soaking time: 2 – 4 hours
Preparation time: 10 minutes
Yields: 2 servings

Preparation Hints

Leave on the white part of the oranges and grapefruit when you peel them to make this a creamier drink.

Ingredient Information

Flax seeds have 24% omega 3 oils, as compared to fish that has 2%. Plus, flax is a mercury-free, toxin-free source of essential fatty acids.

Tangible Life Orange Drink

Citrus is a fruit that is rich in a host of vitamins and minerals. This drink is practically a meal in a glass.

4 tangerines
6 oranges
1 lime
2 Tbsp sunflower seeds
(soaked 8 - 12 hours, rinsed)

Machine Instructions
Put the fine screen over the twin gears. Then attach the pulp discharge casing with the outlet adjusting knob in place, loosening the knob as you juice to allow the pulp to come out. Place the pitcher under the juice outlet to catch the juice, and a bowl under the pulp discharge outlet to catch the pulp.

Preparation and Serving Instructions
1. Peel and cut the tangerines and oranges into pieces that fit into the machine and juice with half the lime (unpeeled).
2. In a blender, mix the soaked sunflower seeds with the juice until smooth and creamy.
3. Serve in a fancy glass, garnished with lime wedges.

Soaking time: 8 - 12 hours
Preparation time: 10 minutes
Yields: 2 servings

Preparation Hints
Rinsing the hulls off the sunflower seeds can be done by adding more water, floating them to the top and pouring them away.

Ingredient Information
Sunflower seeds are rich in calcium, phosphorous and iron as well as vitamins A, D, E and several of the B-complex. Also, they contain a trace amount of fluorine which may account for the claim that they are good for teeth.

In the Pink with Zinc Drink

Pumpkin seeds are high in zinc which is good for preventing prostrate problems and helping feed our immune systems. Cranberries are wonderful for helping our bladders keep in balance. Lemons stimulate the liver to make enzymes. And, apples and bananas have a wide array of vitamins and minerals that support health. This is one of the more satisfying drinks morning, noon or night.

4 apples
1 – 2 bananas
1/2 cup dried cranberries
2 – 4 Tbsp soaked pumpkin seeds
(soaked 8 – 12 hours, rinsed)

1 lemon

Machine Instructions
Put the fine screen over the twin gears. Then attach the pulp discharge casing with the outlet adjusting knob in place, loosening the knob as you juice to allow the pulp to come out. Place the pitcher under the juice outlet to catch the juice, and a bowl under the pulp discharge outlet to catch the pulp.

Preparation and Serving Instructions
1. Cut the apples into pieces that fit into the machine and juice.
2. In a blender, mix until smooth the soaked pumpkin seeds with the apple juice, banana(s) and dried cranberries. Then add lemon juice to taste.
3. Serve in a fancy glass, garnished with lemon wedges.

Soaking time: 8 - 12 hours
Preparation time: 10 minutes
Yields: 2 - 4 servings

Preparation Hints
Keep blending until the drink is thoroughly smooth. To make a thicker drink, add more bananas. To thin, add more apple juice or water.

Pro Bone O' Drink

This drink gives you a plethora of ingredients that help build stronger bones.
Also, the sunflower seeds are a rich source of calcium.

6 oranges

1/2 lime

2 Tbsp flax seeds
(soaked 2 – 4 hours, no rinsing necessary)

3 Tbsp sunflower seeds
(soaked 8 – 12 hours, rinsed)

Machine Instructions

Put the fine screen over the twin gears. Then attach the pulp discharge casing with the outlet adjusting knob in place, loosening the knob as you juice to allow the pulp to come out. Place the pitcher under the juice outlet to catch the juice, and a bowl under the pulp discharge outlet to catch the pulp.

Preparation and Serving Instructions

1. Peel and cut the oranges into pieces that fit into the machine and juice.
2. In a blender, mix the soaked flax seeds and sunflower seeds with the juice until smooth and creamy.

3. Serve in a fancy glass, garnished with orange wedges.

Soaking time: 8 – 12 hours
Preparation time: 10 minutes
Yields: 2 servings

Preparation Hints

Blend with less juice at first, until the mixture is creamy. Then add the rest of the ingredients and thoroughly blend.

Ingredient Information

Sunflower seeds are rich in protein as well as calcium. There are six grams of protein in one tablespoon of sunflower seeds. What a deal!

Orange You Glad It's Grapefruit?

Greens blend well with flax and make for a
healthy drink. I have enjoyed
this juice for many a breakfast.

8 oranges
2 Tbsp flax seeds
(soaked 2 – 4 hours, no rinsing necessary)
2 romaine leaves

Machine Instructions
Put the fine screen over the twin gears. Then
attach the pulp discharge casing with the outlet
adjusting knob in place, loosening the knob as
you juice to allow the pulp to come out. Place the
pitcher under the juice outlet to catch the juice,
and a bowl under the pulp discharge outlet to
catch the pulp.

Preparation and Serving Instructions
1. Peel and cut the oranges into pieces that fit
   into the machine and juice.
2. In a blender, mix the soaked flax seeds and
   romaine leaves with the juice.
3. Serve in a fancy glass, garnished with orange
   slices.

Soaking time: 2 – 4 hours
Preparation time: 10 minutes
Yields: 2 servings

Preparation Hints
Blend with only a small amount of juice initially,
until the seeds and lettuce are well combined.
Then add the rest of the ingredients. On a hot
day, an ice cube or two makes this a cool
refreshing drink.

Ingredient Information
Simply put, this is a healthy drink for your blood,
your brain and your intestines. A great way to
start the day!

Open Sesame Drink

This drink is for adventuresome people. You
need to love a bitter taste to enjoy this drink.

3 grapefruit
1 lemon
1 fresh anise stalk
2 – 3 Tbsp soaked sesame seeds
(soaked 8 –- 12 hours, rinsed)

Machine Instructions
Put the fine screen over the twin gears. Then
attach the pulp discharge casing with the outlet
adjusting knob in place, loosening the knob as
you juice to allow the pulp to come out. Place the
pitcher under the juice outlet to catch the juice,
and a bowl under the pulp discharge outlet to
catch the pulp.

Preparation and Serving Instructions
1. Peel and cut the grapefruit and cut the anise
   and half of the lemon into pieces that fit into
   the machine and juice.
2. In a blender, mix the soaked sesame seeds
   and juice.
3. Serve in a fancy glass, garnished with the wispy
   part of the anise stalk. Using the other half of
   the lemon, squeeze in a bit of fresh lemon juice
   to each glass.

Soaking time: 8 – 12 hours
Preparation time: 10 minutes
Yields: 2 servings

Preparation Hints
Mix some of the sesame seeds with a small
amount of juice first and thoroughly blend. Then
add the rest of the seeds and juice, and blend.

Ingredient Information
Sesame seeds are rich in calcium. In fact, their
calcium content is touted for being as high as
milk but without the problems associated with
dairy products—unwanted hormones, steroids
and antibiotics.

Chapter IV
Frubet

55	**Blushing Frubet** strawberries, dried guava		**Southwestern Slush** apple, banana, raisin	
	Coconut Cream Frubet banana, dried pineapple, coconut milk		**Summer Slush** pineapple, mango, lemon	
	Creamy Mango Frubet mango, banana, lime		**Fall Frubet** persimmons, banana, cranberries	
	Desert Frubet banana, date, dried apricot		**Winter Frubet** orange, cranberry, banana, dates	
	Tropical Frubet pineapple, papaya, coconut milk	**56**	**Northwestern Frubet** blueberry, banana, date, lemon	
	Spring Frubet nectarine, dates, banana, lime		**Lemon Cream Frubet** banana, lemon	

This section combines dried, fresh and frozen fruit into a sauce-like sorbet, hence the name frubet (pronounced frew-bay). The idea for this type of dessert or breakfast came about during a trade show in Las Vegas. We were making sorbet (See Chapter XI – Besserts) combining frozen strawberries with frozen bananas and we ran out of frozen bananas. I was watching the strawberries turn to slush before my eyes, so I decided to combine them with a dried fruit. What a taste treat! Whether you like it fresh or quite frozen, or served as a sauce with fruit salads, you will enjoy this delightful dish.

As with most sweets, personal taste differs, so I am making proportional suggestions at the beginning of this section. You can decide if it is sweet enough, or change it if you want to add more of any one ingredient. Also, for this entire section the machine instructions are the same, as are the preparation instructions. I am sure once you have tried a few of these recipes you will easily come up with your own recipe ideas - variations on a theme.

All Frubet Recipes

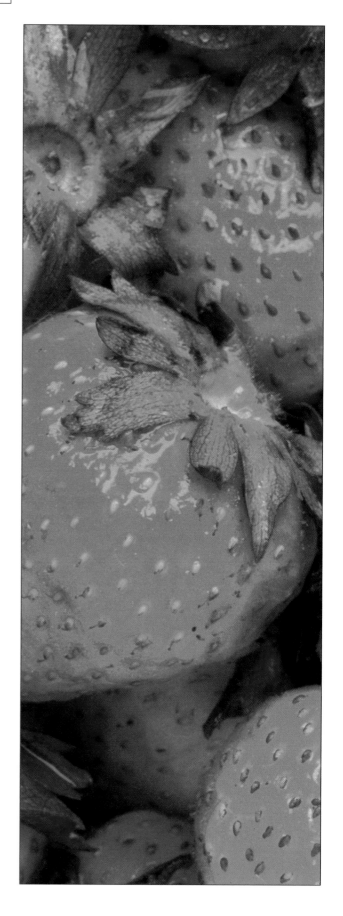

Ingredient Proportions
2 cups frozen fruit (about 4 bananas)
1/2 – 1 cup dried fruit (cut up in small pieces)
1/2 – 1 cup of fresh fruit

Recipe Tips
1. When fresh lemon or limes are used, squeeze the juice, and/or stir in the zest (finely grated citrus skin) to taste.
2. When frozen and/or fresh are called for, try two of each ingredient(e.g. two fresh and two frozen bananas).
3. When frozen or dried ingredients are called for and you prefer dried, make sure to always have at least one frozen fruit per recipe.

Machine Instructions for Frubet Recipes
Put the open blank screen over the twin gears. Then attach the pulp discharge casing without the outlet adjusting knob. Place a large enough bowl to catch any fruit dropping from both the blank opening and the juice outlet. Now, you are ready to prepare a fat-free, cholesterol-free and sugar-free treat.

Preparation and Serving Instructions
1. Freeze fruit, taking off both skins and tops, and place in a plastic bag.
2. Start making the frubet with one cup of the frozen ingredient. Then alternate between ingredients by slowly pushing through a sliced frozen and then a fresh and/or dried fruit, ending with a frozen fruit.
3. Serve as is in a fancy parfait glass or bowl. Or, freeze for 10 to 20 minutes checking for desired consistency.

Preparation time: 10 minutes
Freezing time: 6 – 8 hours
Yields: 2 – 4 servings

Preparation Hints
If you want a sweeter frubet, use more dried fruit. If you want a colder, more sorbet-like dessert, then use more frozen fruit. If you want a more sauce-like consistency, then add more fresh fruit.

Blushing Frubet

frozen strawberries
dried guava

Coconut Cream Frubet

frozen bananas
dried pineapple
(fresh pineapple does not work well,
there is too much pulp)
coconut milk
(To make coconut milk, soak dried coconut—
1 cup coconut to 2 cups water—overnight.
Put through the juicer with the coarse screen.)

Creamy Mango Frubet

frozen or dried mango
fresh and/or frozen bananas
lime juice

Desert Frubet

frozen bananas
pitted dates
dried apricots

Tropical Frubet

frozen or dried pineapple
dried papaya
coconut milk

Spring Frubet

dried and/or fresh nectarines
pitted date
frozen and/or fresh bananas
lime juice

Southwestern Slush

dried and/or fresh apples
raisins (golden or dark)
frozen and/or fresh bananas

Summer Slush

dried or frozen pineapple
(do not use fresh, too much pulp)
frozen or dried mango
lemon juice
lemon zest

Fall Frubet

fresh or frozen persimmons
fresh and/or frozen bananas
dried cranberries

Winter Frubet

fresh pitted dates
fresh orange
dried cranberries
frozen bananas

Northwestern Frubet

frozen blueberries
frozen and/or fresh bananas
pitted dates
lemon juice
lemon zest

Lemon Cream Frubet

frozen bananas
lemon juice
lemon zest

Chapter V
Slurpy Fruit Soups

Spring, summer and fall allow you to experience a wealth of fruits and flavors that make these recipes especially refreshing and satisfying. Using the fruit juice as a stock, the whole fruit can be cut into it or blended, depending on the consistency you prefer. If you want a creamier soup, blend part of the stock, add a banana, almonds or cashews, and thoroughly mix. Fruits tend to digest best by themselves, but for those of us who cannot tolerate a lot of fruit sugar, balance the sugar with soaked nuts or seeds.

When the nuts and seeds are soaked they start to sprout, and lose their coating. Enzyme inhibitors are rinsed away with the soaking water, and the nuts and seeds are easier to digest. Plus, the sprouting or germinating process, activated by soaking 8 to 12 hours and then rinsing, makes them more digestible and easier to combine with fruits. The complex carbohydrates and proteins from these foods can slow down digestion and help our system slow the absorption of the fruit sugar.

Berry Refreshing Soup

This calcium rich broth, orange juice combined with the fresh berries, is such a delicacy. Depending on which berries are chosen, and please feel free to add more than one kind, these soups can really give your mouth a burst of the summer's best flavors.

6 oranges

2 limes

1 box fresh berries

(strawberries, blackberries, raspberries or blueberries)

spearmint

Machine Instructions

Put the fine screen over the twin gears. Then attach the pulp discharge casing with the outlet adjusting knob in place, loosening the knob as you juice to allow the pulp to come out. Place the pitcher under the juice outlet to catch the juice, and a bowl under the pulp discharge outlet to catch the pulp.

Preparation and Serving Instructions

1. Juice peeled oranges and 1/2 lime, unpeeled.
2. Pour fresh berries into mixture.
3. Serve in bowls, garnished with fresh spearmint leaves.

Preparation time: 15 minutes
Yields: 2 servings

Preparation Hints

The juice will come out a bit frothy from the juicer. If you want to reduce the foam, simply stir the soup and then add the fresh fruit pieces.

Sweet Limey Soup

This is citrus heaven for those who like tangerines and limes. The grapes add a crunchy texture to this simple and elegant soup.

4 tangelos

4 tangerines

1 lime

1 bunch of grapes

Machine Instructions

Put the coarse screen over the twin gears. Then attach the pulp discharge casing with the outlet adjusting knob snugly in place. Place the pitcher under the juice outlet to catch the juice, and a bowl under the pulp discharge outlet to catch the pulp.

Preparation and Serving Instructions

1. To make the broth, juice 3 peeled tangelos, 3 peeled tangerines and 1/4 of the lime (unpeeled).
2. Slice the remaining tangelo and tangerine into the broth.
3. Float the grapes and lime slices on top of the soup.
4. Serve in a fancy bowl.

Preparation time: 15 minutes
Yields: 4 servings

Preparation Hints

To add more color to this soup, use different colored grapes. They can be sliced in half to make a fun shape and are easier to eat than if they are whole.

Island Paradise Soup

There is something wildly delicious about this combination of flavors. The sweetness of the pineapple contrasted by the saltiness of the celery just starts the flavor carousel. Then adding the grapes and mango purée with pineapple pieces makes a tropical paradise. The crunchiness of the grape, the smoothness of the mango purée and the sweetness of the pineapple—wow!

2 celery
1/2 pineapple
2 cups purple grapes
1 cup mango puree

Machine Instructions
Put the fine screen over the twin gears. Then attach the pulp discharge casing with the outlet adjusting knob in place, loosening the knob as you juice to allow the pulp to come out. Place the pitcher under the juice outlet to catch the juice, and a bowl under the pulp discharge outlet to catch the pulp.

Preparation and Serving Instructions
1. To make the broth, juice celery and peeled pineapple, leaving 2 pineapple slices for the soup.
2. Pour mango purée in a circle around the pineapple juice, adding grapes and pineapple slices to the broth.
3. Serve in lovely bowls.

Preparation time: 15 minutes
Yields: 2 servings

Preparation Hints
Slicing the pineapple into rings and then vertically to fit into the juicer makes the juicing easier. The celery gives a salty flavor, so start with one piece of celery and taste. Add more celery if desired.

Peachy Keen Soup

The spearmint in this soup adds sparkle to the flavor of the peaches and strawberries.
Be sure to enjoy its unique taste.

1 box strawberries

3 bananas

2 peaches

2 – 4 spearmint leaves

Machine Instructions

Put the open blank screen over the twin gears. Then attach the pulp discharge casing without the outlet adjusting knob. Place a large enough bowl to catch any droppings from both the blank opening and the juice outlet.

Preparation and Serving Instructions

1. To make soup broth, alternate putting 2 bananas, fresh or frozen with 1/2 box of fresh strawberries through the machine. Pour into a bowl.
2. Float strawberries, banana and peach slices in the broth.

3. Serve in a fancy bowl, garnished with spearmint leaves.

Freezing time: 6 – 8 hours
Preparation time: 10 minutes
Yields: 2 servings

Preparation Hints

On a those hot summer days when you want something cool to enjoy, with very little effort this soup can be transformed to a cool treat. Freeze the bananas and put them through the machine with the fresh strawberries. This combination makes the broth similar to a slush.

Plum Good Soup

The summer fruits are such fun to combine. This soup tastes almost like a lemonade. Remember though, when juicing a little lemon goes a long way.

4 apples

1 lemon

2 nectarines

2 plums

Machine Instructions

Put the fine screen over the twin gears. Then attach the pulp discharge casing with the outlet adjusting knob in place, loosening the knob as you juice to allow the pulp to come out. Place the pitcher under the juice outlet to catch the juice, and a bowl under the pulp discharge outlet to catch the pulp.

Preparation and Serving Instructions

1. To make the broth, juice 3 apples and 1/4 lemon with the rind.
2. In a blender, finish making the broth by blending apple juice with 1 nectarine.
3. Float plum, nectarine and apple slices in the broth.
4. Serve in a fancy bowl, garnished with apple and lemon slices.

Preparation time: 15 minutes
Yields: 2 servings

Preparation Hints

Fujis are the best apples to juice, otherwise make sure it is a firm and crisp apple. For those who find plums' skin too tart, peel it. Otherwise, enjoy the contrast of the sweet and sour.

Blueberriest Soup

This drink is like a smoothie and a soup combined. I love seeing the brightness of the color combination, and the lovely burst of blueberry flavor.

3 cups apple juice

3 bananas

1 box blueberries

Machine Instructions

Put the fine screen over the twin gears. Then put the pulp discharge casing with the outlet adjusting knob in place, loosening as you juice to allow the pulp to come out. Place the pitcher under the screen opening to catch the juice, and a bowl under the outlet adjusting knob to catch the pulp.

Preparation and Serving Instructions

1. Juice apples (about 8 - 10 apples will make 3 cups).
2. In a blender, make stock by blending apple juice with 2 bananas.
3. Float blueberries, banana and apple slices in stock.
4. Serve in a fancy bowl, garnished with apple slices.

Preparation time: 15 minutes
Yields: 2 servings

Preparation Hints

Fujis are the best apples to juice. Otherwise use crisp apples. If the machine starts making apple sauce, loosen the outlet adjusting knob. If that does not help, then stop the machine, clean the screen, reassemble and start again.

Green Goddess Soup

I was so excited when I discovered this taste combination. Avocado is a fruit and as such combines perfectly with the sweet nectar of the orange, and is contrasted by the sourness of the grapefruit. Delightful!

1 grapefruit

3 oranges

1 avocado

Machine Instructions

Put the fine screen over the twin gears. Then attach the pulp discharge casing with the outlet adjusting knob in place, loosening the knob as you juice to allow the pulp to come out. Place the pitcher under the juice outlet to catch the juice, and a bowl under the pulp discharge outlet to catch the pulp.

Preparation and Serving Instructions

1. To make the broth, juice 2 peeled oranges, and 3/4 peeled grapefruit.
2. Slice avocado, one orange and the remainder of the grapefruit into the broth.
3. Serve in bowls, garnished with the orange rind.

Preparation time: 15 minutes
Yields: 2 servings

Preparation Hints

Pink grapefruit is a lovely alternative to the standard yellow color.

Holiday Delight Soup

The festive colors of this soup make it a holiday favorite for guests around my home. Strawberries have a natural painkiller, salicylate, and so this drink helps relieve any stress celebrating may create.

6 oranges
4 kiwi
1 box fresh strawberries

Machine Instructions
Put the fine screen over the twin gears. Then attach the pulp discharge casing with the outlet adjusting knob in place, loosening the knob as you juice to allow the pulp to come out. Place the pitcher under the juice outlet to catch the juice, and a bowl under the pulp discharge outlet to catch the pulp.

Preparation and Serving Instructions
1. Juice peeled oranges.
2. To make the broth, in a blender mix kiwis and orange juice.
3. Slice 2 kiwis and the strawberries into the broth.
4. Serve in bowls, garnished with fresh strawberries.

Preparation time: 15 minutes
Yields: 4 servings

Preparation Hints
The colors and shapes of the kiwis and strawberries lend themselves easily to decorating. Play with different shapes and come up with your favorites. Playing with food can be so creative and satisfying.

Raspberry Cream Soup

Cashews are great with orange juice and make the creamiest texture. I love this soup on a warm day, or as a dip for parties. Another fun idea is to serve it as a fondue with the soup in the middle and the fruit arranged around it on a platter.

3 cups orange juice
(about 8 – 12 oranges)
1 1/2 cups raw cashews
1 box raspberries
1 orange

Machine Instructions
Put the fine screen over the twin gears. Then attach the pulp discharge casing with the outlet adjusting knob in place, loosening the knob as you juice to allow the pulp to come out. Place the pitcher under the juice outlet to catch the juice, and a bowl under the pulp discharge outlet to catch the pulp.

Preparation and Serving Instructions
1. Juice peeled oranges.
2. In a blender, make stock by blending orange juice with the cashews, adding half the box of raspberries last.
3. Float raspberries and orange slices in the broth.
4. Serve in a fancy bowl, garnished with orange slices.

Preparation time: 15 minutes
Yields: 2 servings

Preparation Hints
If you want a thicker broth, start out blending with less juice than nuts and add the last cup of juice slowly until the desired consistency is achieved.

Chapter VI

Do You Carrot All for Vegetable Soup?

This section is filled with vegetable soup ideas that you can do in a jiffy. From juice to crunchy mixtures, these meals in a bowl can be quite filling. Serving soups with a green leafy salad and crackers or dehydrated breads makes an entirely satisfying meal.

Steamy Basil Soup

As simple to make as it is delicious to eat. Find different kinds of basil and experiment with their flavors. There is a purple basil, a cinnamon basil, a green Italian and a curly leafed basil. So you have a world of delightful choices.

2 cups fresh carrot juice

1 avocado

6 – 10 fresh basil leaves

1 lemon

Machine Instructions

Put the fine screen over the twin gears. Then attach the pulp discharge casing with the outlet adjusting knob snugly in place. Place the pitcher under the juice outlet to catch the juice and a bowl under the pulp discharge outlet to catch any pulp.

Preparation and Serving Instructions

1. To make the broth, juice carrots.
2. In a blender, mix carrot juice, avocado and basil leaves together, spicing to taste.
3. Serve in a lovely bowl or cup, garnished with lemon slices and a fresh basil leaf.

Preparation time: 25 minutes
Yields: 4 – 6 servings

Corny Soup

What makes this soup special is the fresh corn with the ginger, in a creamy base. You can make this soup as smooth or as crunchy as you like—diner's choice.

4 cups fresh carrot juice
1 avocado
1 – 2 slices fresh ginger root
2 ears fresh white corn
1 lime
Bragg's liquid aminos

Machine Instructions

Put the fine screen over the twin gears. Then attach the pulp discharge casing with the outlet adjusting knob snugly in place. Place the pitcher under the juice outlet to catch the juice, and a bowl under the pulp discharge outlet to catch any pulp.

Preparation and Serving Instructions

1. To make the broth, juice carrots.
2. In blender, mix carrot juice, avocado and spice with the ginger root to taste. Add corn last and blend to desired smoothness.
3. Serve in a lovely bowl or cup, spicing with lime juice and Bragg's to taste. Garnish with lime and a slice of fresh ginger.

Preparation time: 20 minutes
Yields: 4 – 6 servings

Preparation Hints

Have fun experimenting with the consistency of this soup. It can be two distinct kinds of soup — chewy one day, slurpy the next.

Darn Grate Soup

The calcium-rich soup's delightful flavor is from the jicama and yams with the carrots and celery. The apple, carrots and jicama make it without the need of artificial sweeteners.

Broth
6 – 8 carrots
1 apple
2 celery stalks
3/4 peeled jicama
1/2 yam

Soup fillings
1 carrot
1 celery stalk
1/4 peeled jicama
1/2 yam
parsley

Machine Instructions

Put the fine screen over the twin gears. Then attach the pulp discharge casing with the outlet adjusting knob snugly in place. Place the pitcher under the screen opening to catch the juice, and a bowl under the outlet adjusting knob to catch the pulp.

Preparation and Serving Instructions

1. To make the broth, juice 4 carrots, 1 apple, 2 celery stalks, and 1/4 peeled jicama together.
2. To thicken broth, in a blender mix 2 carrots, half the jicama and half the yam.
3. Put 1 stalk of finely diced celery, and finely grated 1/2 yam, 1/4 peeled jicama, and 1 finely grated carrot into a bowl.
4. Pour broth over vegetables, garnishing with parsley.

Preparation time: 20 minutes
Yields: 4 – 6 servings

Preparation Hints

If you prefer a lighter soup with a thinner consistency, the broth can be more liquid by eliminating step two. Otherwise, enjoy the textures of the broth and the grated vegetables.

Blushing Borscht

This is a soup of contrasts: crunchy and smooth, sweet and tart. The avocado topping is creamy, the grated vegetables give your jaw a gentle workout. I enjoy the juicy sweetness of the carrots, beets and apples contrasted with the tartness of the lemon juice.

Broth

2 cups carrot juice (8 – 10 carrots)

1/2 cup beet juice (2 – 3 beets)

1/4 cup apple juice (3 – 5 apples)

1 lemon

Soup fillings

2 beets

1 cup purple cabbage, finely chopped

1 carrot

2 green onions

1 cup fresh dill weed

Topping

1 avocado

1 celery stalk

1 lemon

Bragg's liquid aminos

Machine Instructions

Put the fine screen over the twin gears. Then attach the pulp discharge casing with the outlet adjusting knob snugly in place. Place the pitcher under the juice outlet to catch the juice, and a bowl under the outlet adjusting knob to catch any pulp.

Preparation and Serving Instructions

1. To make the broth, juice carrots, beets, apples and 1/4 lemon with peel.
2. In a blender, mix dill weed, 1 green onion with broth, spicing with Bragg's and lemon juice to taste.
3. Put finely grated beets, carrot and cabbage into broth, adding finely chopped dill weed last.
4. To make topping, in a blender mix avocado, 1 green onion and celery, seasoning with lemon juice and Bragg's to taste.
5. Garnish soup with topping and fresh dill.

Preparation time: 25 minutes
Yields: 4 – 6 servings

Preparation Hints

There is a European grater I like to use for this recipe to give the beets and carrots a juiced consistency. For more information on this grater, see the Resources section.

Christmas Delight Soup

This soup is a holiday favorite: the dark, rich red of the tomatoes and purple cabbage contrasted by the bright green of the parsley, basil and green cabbage. To serve it at Christmas find green house tomatoes. Or, serve it in the fall when tomatoes are the most flavorful.

Broth

1 cup purple cabbage

6 – 8 large red tomatoes

Soup fillings

6 fresh basil leaves

1/2 cup fresh parsley

1 cup green cabbage, chopped

2 limes

Machine Instructions

Put the open blank screen over the twin gears. Then attach the pulp discharge casing without the outlet adjusting knob. Place a large enough bowl to catch any droppings from both the blank opening and the pulp discharge outlet.

Preparation and Serving Instructions

1. To make soup broth, alternate putting fresh red tomatoes and purple cabbage through the machine and into a bowl. Stir with a whisk to blend the flavors.
2. Pour water through the machine to clear out the tomato or rinse out the housing and twin gears and reassemble. Then put basil, parsley and green cabbage through the machine and into a separate bowl.
3. Serve in a bowl. First pour in the red mixture and then the green mixture on top in a ring.
4. Garnish with tomato and lime slices, with parsley and basil on top of the slices.

Preparation time: 25 minutes
Yields: 2 servings

Preparation Hints

Keep the "colors" separate until the soup is served.

Blimey a Limey Tomato Cabbage Soup

This soup is a rainbow of colors. What makes it special is the combination of the tomato and cabbage flavors. The dill and lime add that extra zing. Dill is so great, I put it on almost anything I eat.

Broth

6 – 8 red tomatoes

1/2 purple cabbage

Soup filling

4 – 6 yellow tomatoes

2 limes

12 cherry tomatoes (red and yellow)

1/4 cup fresh dill weed

Machine Instruction

Put the open blank screen over the twin gears. Then attach the pulp discharge casing without the outlet adjusting knob. Place a large enough bowl to catch any droppings from both the blank opening and the pulp discharge outlet and you are ready to prepare a thick and rich soup broth.

Preparation and Serving Instructions

1. To make soup broth, alternate putting fresh red tomatoes, cabbage and fresh dill weed through the machine and into a bowl. Stir with a whisk to blend all the flavors.
2. Pour water through the machine to clear out the red tomato or rinse out the housing and the twin gears and reassemble. Then put the yellow tomatoes through the machine and into a separate bowl.
3. Prepare by first pouring the red mixture into the bowl, then the yellow on top and in a ring.
4. Garnish with lime slices, cherry tomatoes sliced in half and sprigs of fresh dill.

Preparation time: 25 minutes
Yields: 4 servings

Preparation Hints

For those who would prefer, this soup can be made with only red tomatoes and green cabbage can be substituted for purple. Also, lemon can be exchanged for lime.

Asparagusto Soup

With its red middle, ring of bright yellow and green, red and yellow topping, this soup is one of the prettiest soups to serve.

Broth
6 – 8 red tomatoes, large
4 – 6 dried tomatoes
1 bunch of asparagus (save tips as garnish)
4 – 8 fresh basil leaves

Soup fillings
4 – 6 yellow tomatoes
1/2 cup of fresh parsley
1 lime

Machine Instructions
Put the open blank screen over the twin gears. Then attach the pulp discharge casing without the outlet adjusting knob. Place a large enough bowl to catch any droppings from both the blank opening and the pulp discharge outlet.

Preparation and Serving Instructions
1. To make soup broth, alternate putting fresh red tomatoes and dried tomatoes, basil and asparagus stalks (save the tips) through the machine, into a bowl. Stir with a whisk to blend the flavors. Save one red and one yellow tomato for garnishing.
2. To clear out the red tomato, pour water through the machine or rinse the housing and twin gears, and reassemble. Then put the yellow tomatoes through the machine and into a separate bowl.
3. Serve in soups bowls. Put a slice of lime in each bowl and pour in the red mixture. Then pour the yellow mixture around the top in a ring.
4. Garnish with lime, basil, parsley, red and yellow tomato slices and raw asparagus tips.

Preparation time: 25 minutes
Yields: 4 servings

Preparation Hints
Use sweet tasting tomatoes. Otherwise, the spices need make up the difference in the flavor.

Chunky Veggie Soup

This soup could be called Summer Stock for its array of ingredients. The sweet corn, salty celery, bitter arugula, creamy broth and flavorful spices give it a richly flavored cast of characters.

Broth
2 – 2-1/2 cups fresh carrot juice
1 avocado
4 – 6 celery stalks
1 lemon

Soup fillings
1 summer squash
2 carrots
2 – 3 ears fresh corn
2 – 4 celery stalks
1 cup arugula

Spice options: parsley, basil or cilantro

Machine Instructions
Put the fine screen over the twin gears. Then attach the pulp discharge casing with the outlet adjusting knob snugly in place. Put the pitcher under the juice outlet to catch the juice and a bowl under the pulp discharge outlet to catch any pulp.

Preparation and Serving Instructions
1. To make the broth, juice carrots.
2. In a blender, mix carrot juice, avocado, 3 – 4 celery stalks (to taste), spicing with lemon juice after it is blended smoothly.
3. Add finely grated squash, carrots and corn (cut off the cob), with finely diced celery and finely chopped arugula. Add other fresh green spices last.
4. Serve in a lovely bowl or cup, garnished with lemon slices and fresh herbs.

Preparation time: 25 minutes
Yields: 4 – 6 servings

Preparation Hints
The multi-slicer or other mandolin-type tool is useful for cutting the corn off the cob. Otherwise, a sharp knife and the cob slanted into a bowl, does the trick.

Chapter VII
Saucing It Up with Fruits

These sauces are delicious over fresh fruits, frozen fruit desserts, fruit pies, sprouts or salad greens. To make them thicker, add more bananas. To make it thinner, add more of the other fruits. I have enjoyed these sauces inside fruit rolls as crêpe stuffing. As you experiment, you will come up with many uses for these tasty, fat-free sweet sauces.

Mango Madness

1 large fresh peeled sliced mango
(or 2 small ones)
2 fresh bananas
1 frozen banana
1 lime

Machine Instructions

Put the open blank screen over the twin gears. Then attach the pulp discharge casing without the outlet adjusting knob. Place a large enough bowl to catch any droppings from both the blank opening and the pulp discharge outlet.

Preparation and Serving Instructions

1. To make the sauce, alternate juicing 2 fresh bananas, and frozen banana with mango slices. Pour into a bowl.
2. Spice with lime juice to taste.
3. Serve in a fancy bowl or on top of fresh fruit or greens.

Freezing time: 6 – 8 hours
Preparation time: 10 minutes
Yields: 2 cups of sauce

Preparation Hints

Slicing the mango can be a messy job. If you slice it on angles, there will be more fruit and less juice while you are preparing it for the sauce.

Bon Apricot Sauce

If you can find Turkish apricots, you are in for a real treat. They are so succulent.

**1 cup dried apricots
or 4 – 6 fresh apricots
2 fresh bananas
1 frozen banana
1 fresh apple
1 lemon**

Machine Instructions

Put the open blank screen over the twin gears. Then attach the pulp discharge casing without the outlet adjusting knob. Place a large enough bowl to catch any droppings from both the blank opening and the pulp discharge outlet.

Preparation and Serving Instructions

1. To make the sauce, alternate putting 2 fresh bananas, and frozen banana with dried or fresh apricots, and apple through the machine and into a bowl.
2. Spice with lemon juice to taste.
3. Serve in a fancy bowl or on top of fresh fruit or greens.

**Freezing time: 6 – 8 hours
Preparation time: 10 minutes
Yields: 2 cups of sauce**

Preparation Hints

You can peel or leave the skin on the apple. If it is a waxed apple, definitely peel it. Otherwise, the skins add a flavor and a texture that some prefer, plus a good deal of nutrition. If the dried apricots are hard, you might want to soak them for a short while in warm water. This will make the sauce a bit creamier.

Creamy Mint Sauce

It is the spearmint that brightens up this special sauce.

**2 fresh bananas
1 frozen banana
1/2 cup fresh spearmint leaves
1 lime**

Machine Instructions

Put the open blank screen over the twin gears. Then attach the pulp discharge casing without the outlet adjusting knob. Place a large enough bowl to catch any droppings from both the blank opening and the pulp discharge outlet.

Preparation and Serving Instructions

1. To make the sauce, alternate putting 2 fresh bananas, and frozen banana with mint leaves through the machine and into a bowl.
2. Spice with lime juice to taste.
3. Serve in a fancy bowl or on top of citrus fruit, strawberries or fresh greens.

**Freezing time: 6 – 8 hours
Preparation time: 10 minutes
Yields: 2 cups sauce**

Preparation Hints

This can be made without the frozen fruit, but it does cool down the sauce if one of the bananas is frozen. The weather might determine your choice.

Cranapple Sauce

The sweetness of the apples, dates and bananas contrasted to the tartness of the lemon juice and cranberries makes this sauce sizzle with taste.

2 fresh bananas
1 frozen banana
3 apples
2 – 4 pitted dates
1/2 cup dried cranberries
1 lemon

Machine Instructions

Put the open blank screen over the twin gears. Then attach the pulp discharge casing without the outlet adjusting knob. Place a large enough bowl to catch any droppings from both the blank opening and the pulp discharge outlet.

Preparation and Serving Instructions

1. To make the sauce, alternate putting 2 fresh bananas, and the frozen banana with apples, pitted dates and dried cranberries through the machine and into a bowl.

2. Spice with lemon juice to taste.
3. Serve in a fancy bowl or on top of fresh fruit or greens.

Freezing time: 6 – 8 hours
Preparation time: 10 minutes
Yields: 2 cups of sauce

Preparation Hints

If the dried cranberries are too hard, soak them in hot water for 20 minutes or so, and then put them through the machine.

Persnickety Persimmon

This fall delight is a true holiday treat. It can even stand on its own as a soup. If you want to serve this sauce during other seasons, make it with only fresh bananas and frozen persimmons.

2 – 4 fresh ripe persimmons
(the soft kind)
2 fresh bananas
1 frozen banana
spices: cinnamon, nutmeg

Machine Instructions
Put the open blank screen over the twin gears. Then attach the pulp discharge casing without the outlet adjusting knob. Place a large enough bowl to catch any droppings from both the blank opening and the pulp discharge outlet.

Preparation and Serving Instructions
1. To make the sauce, alternate putting 2 fresh bananas, and frozen banana with persimmon through the machine and into a bowl.
2. Spice with cinnamon and nutmeg to taste.
3. Serve by itself or on top of fresh fruit or greens.

Freezing time: 6 – 8 hours
Preparation time: 10 minutes
Yields: 2 cups of sauce

Preparation Hints
Make sure you cut off the top of the persimmon. You will want to use ripe persimmons for this sauce, so the persimmon should be soft and squishy, not firm.

Sparkling Blueberry Jello Sauce

When I first made it, I did not know that the blueberries would turn into the consistency of a jello. It wiggles and jiggles and tastes great.

1 box fresh blueberries
2 fresh bananas
1 frozen banana
1 lime

Machine Instructions
Put the open blank screen over the twin gears. Then attach the pulp discharge casing without the outlet adjusting knob. Place a large enough bowl to catch any droppings from both the blank opening and the pulp discharge outlet.

Preparation and Serving Instructions
1. To make the sauce, alternate putting 2 fresh bananas, and frozen banana with blueberries through the machine and into a bowl.
2. Add lime juice to taste.
3. Serve in a fancy bowl or on top of fresh fruit or greens.

Freezing time: 6 – 8 hours
Preparation time: 10 minutes
Yields: 2 cups of sauce

Preparation Hints
This dish can be made year round, by using either fresh or frozen blueberries. When using frozen blueberries, remember that the flavor will not be as strong as freezing does diminish the taste of some fruits.

Raspberried Sauce

Whether you have red or black berries, this sauce is what I call "yumicious" or outrageously delicious. If you want to make this out of season, freeze the berries and use more fresh bananas.

2 boxes of fresh raspberries (black or red are fine)
2 fresh bananas
1 frozen banana

Machine Instructions

Put the open blank screen over the twin gears. Then attach the pulp discharge casing without the outlet adjusting knob. Place a large enough bowl to catch any droppings from both the blanks opening and the pulp discharge outlet.

Preparation and Serving Instructions

1. To make the sauce, alternate putting 2 fresh bananas, and frozen banana with berries through the machine and into a bowl.

2. Serve in a fancy bowl or on top of fresh fruit or greens.

Freezing time: 6 – 8 hours
Preparation time: 10 minutes
Yields: 2 cups of sauce

Preparation Hints

The berries give this sauce a slightly crunchy texture. If you want a creamier texture, you can add more banana.

Simmering Summer Sauce

1 skinned pineapple

1 box fresh strawberries

2 fresh bananas

1 frozen banana

1 – 2 oranges

Machine Instructions

Put the open blank screen over the twin gears. Then attach the pulp discharge casing without the outlet adjusting knob. Place a large enough bowl to catch any droppings from both the blank opening and the pulp discharge outlet.

Preparation and Serving Instructions

1. To make the sauce, alternate putting 2 fresh bananas, and frozen banana with pineapple slices and fresh strawberries through the machine and into a bowl.

2. Add orange juice to taste.

3. Serve in a fancy bowl or on top of fresh fruit or greens.

Freezing time: 6 – 8 hours
Preparation time: 10 minutes
Yields: 2 cups of sauce

Preparation Hints

For a cooler sauce, you can freeze half the strawberries and enjoy it chilled.

Chapter VIII

Dressings: Sauces, Salsas, Seed Cheeses and Dips

Whether you use these dressings on raw or steamed greens, grains or vegetables, or as a dip, they are scrumptious. For a dressing, thin down with more fluids. For a sauce-like consistency, thicken by using less fluids or more dried ingredients. I have enjoyed the tomato sauce over grated squash or cooked noodles. The combination of the raw with the cooked gives you more enzymes to help digest the cooked food. You can warm up some of these dressings by using a skillet, on low heat, or an electric skillet on warm. Use your finger as a guide, not letting the skillet get too hot to touch. Otherwise, these can be served fresh or chilled, if desired. Choices, choices, choices.

Stephen's Apple Flaxed Dressing

This recipe idea was shared with me by Stephen Case while we were working together in Vancouver, photographing the recipes in this book. Siegfried added flax oil to the list of ingredients, and this recipe is the result. Full of essential fatty acids, flax oil is one of the healthiest oils for our bodies.

1 cup apple juice (5 – 7 apples)
1/4 – 1/2 cup fennel juice (3 – 6 stalks)
1/4 – 1/2 cup lemon juice (2 – 3 lemons)
1/4 – 1/2 cup flax oil
2 – 4 tsp fennel stalk, finely diced
(the wispy part of the stalk)

Machine Instructions

Put the fine screen over the twin gears. Then attach the pulp discharge casing with the outlet adjusting knob in place, loosening the knob as you juice to allow the pulp to come out. Place the pitcher under the juice outlet to catch the juice and a bowl under the pulp discharge outlet to catch the pulp.

Preparation and Serving Instructions

1. Cut up the apples, fennel and lemons into pieces that fit into the machine and juice, measuring each ingredient's juice, or put it all together and juice to desired taste.
2. Stir the flax oil into the juice mixture: start with 1/4 cup and add the proportions to taste.
3. Finely dice the wispy part of the fennel stalk and let marinate in the dressing for 30 minutes or so before serving.

Preparation time: 10 minutes
Yields: 2 cups of dressing

Preparation Hints

The anise and lemon juice have such strong flavors so juice to taste, or juice separately and blend together to taste. There are several varieties of flax seed oil in the refrigerator section of most natural food stores. Find the one you like as they all have a slightly different taste.

Better Beet Dressing

This red dressing is protein and calcium-rich, making it a favorite for building strong bones.

2 – 4 beets (1/2 cup of juice)
1 cup soaked sunflower seeds
Bragg's liquid aminos
1 lemon

Machine Instructions (For the juicing)

Put the fine screen over the twin gears. Then attach the pulp discharge casing with the outlet adjusting knob snugly in place. Put the pitcher under the juice outlet to catch the juice and a bowl under the pulp discharge outlet to catch any pulp.

Machine Instructions (For making the sauce)

Rinse parts and exchange the fine screen for the open blank screen and slide it over the twin gears. Then attach the pulp discharge casing without the outlet adjusting knob. Place a large enough bowl to catch any droppings from both the blank opening and the pulp discharge outlet.

Preparation and Serving Instructions

1. Soak sunflower seeds for 8 – 12 hours, rinse and drain.
2. Juice the beets.
3. Change the screen to the open blank, and alternate putting the sunflower seeds and beet juice through the machine and into a bowl.
4. Stir the mixture, spicing with lemon juice and Bragg's to taste.
5. Serve as a dip or tossed over salads, loaves, grains or vegetables.

Soaking Time: 8 – 12 hours
Preparation time: 10 minutes
Yields: 1-1/2 cups

Preparation Hints

To remove the sunflower seed hulls after soaking fill the container that the seeds have soaked in with twice as much water as seeds. The hulls float to the top and can be poured out. Repeat until most of the hulls have been rinsed away. Or, skim the hulls off the top with a strainer or fine mesh spoon. Beet juice can have a strong flavor, so modify the amounts to suit your tastes.

Creamy Thousand Island Dressing

Usually this type of dressing uses eggs, lots of oil and sugar. Not exactly healthy! Instead, this recipe uses pine nuts which have a delightful flavor and are rich in essential oils making this dressing delicious, creamy and healthy.

3/4 – 1 cup pine nuts

1/4 cup fresh lemon juice

2 fresh tomatoes

2 – 4 Tbsp tapenade

6 – 8 fresh basil leaves

1/2 cup fresh parsley

2 celery stalks

Bragg's liquid aminos

1 Tbsp Tomato Delight

Machine Instructions

Put the open blank screen over the twin gears. Then attach the pulp discharge casing without the outlet adjusting knob. Put the pitcher under the juice outlet to catch the juice and a bowl under the pulp discharge outlet to catch the pulp.

Preparation and Serving Instructions

1. Alternate putting the ingredients through the machine and into a bowl.
2. Stir the mixture, spicing with Tomato Delight, lemon juice and Bragg's to taste.
3. Serve as a dip or tossed over salads, loaves, grains or vegetables.

Preparation time: 10 minutes
Yields: 2 cups

Preparation Hints

Tapenade is a dehydrated tomato paste, with olive oil and garlic. This product can be found in most natural food stores. Tomato Delight is a dehydrated tomato powdered spice. If these products are unavailable, the sauce can be made by substituting those ingredients with fresh garlic cloves and dried tomatoes.

Presto Pesto

Traditionally, this recipe calls for dairy products and a lot of oil. I make mine with a mixture of parsley and basil, making this sauce even greener, and without any dairy. Feel free to take out the olive oil and add avocado which makes for a creamy recipe as well.

1 cup fresh basil

1 cup fresh parsley

1 – 2 cloves of garlic

1 cup walnuts

1 lemon

2 Tbsp olive oil (or 1 avocado)

Bragg's liquid aminos

Machine Instructions
Put the open blank screen over the twin gears. Then attach the pulp discharge casing without the outlet adjusting knob. Place a large enough bowl to catch any droppings from both the blank opening and the pulp discharge outlet.

Preparation and Serving Instructions
1. Alternate putting the basil, parsley, garlic, walnuts and olive oil through the machine and into a bowl.
2. Stir the mixture, spicing with lemon juice and Bragg's to taste.
3. Serve as a dip or over salads, baked potatoes or squash. Or, use on pizza instead of tomato sauce.

Preparation time: 10 minutes
Yields: 2 cups

Preparation Hints
Let the machine pull the parsley and basil through itself. This happens easiest when the chute is empty and the gears are clear. Likewise, the walnuts will go through easier when put in slowly, a small amount at a time.

Sunrise Seed Cheeses

These "cheeses" are a brilliantly colored, tangy flavored treat. Whether you serve on a cracker or vegetable chip, this fermented dip is a festive addition to any party. Also, it is good source of natural acidophilus.

Basic cheese
1 – 2 tsp red miso
2 cups sunflower seeds
Use 2 cups of the basic cheese for each color cheese desired.

For Golden Yellow
1/2 – 1 tsp turmeric
1/2 – 1 tsp curry powder
1 yellow bell pepper

For Blushing Crimson
1 red bell pepper
1 small beet
1/2 – 1 tsp paprika

For Garden Green
1 green bell pepper
1/4 cup fresh parsley
6 – 8 fresh basil leaves

Machine Instructions
Put the closed blank screen over the twin gears. Then attach the pulp discharge casing without the outlet adjusting knob. Place a bowl to catch the droppings from the pulp discharge outlet and you are ready to prepare a zesty seed cheese.

Preparation and Serving Instructions
1. To make the basic seed cheese, soak the sunflower seeds 8 – 12 hours and rinse, leaving some water in the container. Put this through the machine, with miso and some of the rinsing water. Pour this mixture into a cotton bag, strain out liquid and serve, or chill and store. Or, to ferment, pour this mixture into a glass jar and let sit on the counter overnight, or until fermented (8 – 12 hours). The whey will settle to the bottom and separate from the cheese.
2. To make Golden Yellow seed cheese, prepare the basic recipe, putting yellow bell pepper through the machine with the sunflower seeds, water and miso. Stir the turmeric and curry powder into the mixture to taste. Strain and serve or let sit as above until fermented.
3. To make Blushing Crimson seed cheese, prepare the basic recipe, putting beet and red bell pepper through the machine with the sunflower seeds, water and miso. Stir the paprika into the mixture to taste. Strain and serve or let sit as above until fermented.
4. For the Garden Green seed cheese, prepare the basic recipe, putting parsley, basil and green bell pepper through the machine with the sunflower seeds, water and miso to taste. Strain and serve or let sit as above until fermented.

Soaking time: 8 – 12 hours
Preparation time: 10 minutes for each cheese
Fermenting time: 8 – 12 hours
Yields: 2 – 3 cups seed cheese each color

Preparation Hints
When making the seed cheese, do pour some water into the machine while blending, about 2 – 4 tablespoons is fine. These cheeses can be drained and pressed into a firmer seed cheese by draining off the whey (the liquid that settles to the bottom) and pressing the cheese into a cotton bag, or finely meshed natural fabric before or after fermenting. Let it hang to drain, and store in the refrigerator. Either texture can be served with veggie chips or crackers.

Such a Sweet Sauce

I first encountered this sauce during a show I was doing with a raw food chef and good friend named Adia. We were making an almond carrot loaf and this sauce went on top. The sweetness from the dates is reminiscent of the tomato sauces sweetened with sugar, but this is much more palatable.

3 fresh tomatoes

1 cup dried tomatoes

1/4 cup fresh basil

1 garlic clove

2 – 4 pitted dates

2 Tbsp extra virgin olive oil

1 lemon

Machine Instructions
Put the open blank screen over the twin gears. Then attach the pulp discharge casing without the outlet adjusting knob. Place a large enough bowl to catch any droppings from both the blank opening and the pulp discharge outlet.

Preparation and Serving Instructions
1. Alternate putting the fresh and dried tomatoes, green onions, garlic and pitted dates through the machine and into a bowl.
2. Stir the mixture adding the olive oil, spicing with lemon juice to taste.
3. Serve chilled or as a dip. Delicious as a sauce for nut loaves, vegetables or noodles.

Preparation time: 10 minutes
Yields: 2 cups

Preparation Hints
A thinner sauce can be made by adding more fresh tomatoes, a thicker one by adding more dried tomatoes. The flower from the basil is a wonderful flavor, do not throw it out while rinsing. Extra virgin olive oil, touted as keeping Italians free from heart disease, is perhaps the healthiest addition to this sauce.

Italian Eggplant Sauce

This recipe a great spread for tortillas or pita pockets. It is thought that eggplant has to be cooked to eat it, but this is not so. This sauce can be made entirely raw, and it tastes great. It also goes well with other Middle Eastern dishes like tabouli (a cracked wheat salad) or tahini (sesame butter). This sauce's slightly bitter flavor makes it wonderful for salads.

1 peeled eggplant

4 – 6 dried tomatoes

1/4 cup fresh parsley

1 – 2 garlic cloves

2 – 3 tsp raw tahini

1 – 2 limes

Jensen's Quick Sip, Soy Sauce or Bragg's liquid aminos

Machine Instructions
Put the open blank screen over the twin gears. Then attach the pulp discharge casing without the outlet adjusting knob. Place a large enough bowl to catch any droppings from both the blank opening and the pulp discharge outlet.

Preparation and Serving Instructions
1. Alternate putting the peeled sliced eggplant, dried tomatoes, parsley and garlic through the machine and into a bowl.
2. Thin the tahini with 1 or 2 teaspoons of water first and then stir into the mixture, spicing with lime juice and Jensen's, soy sauce or Bragg's to taste. (Add less tahini, taste and then add more if desired.)
3. Serve as a dip with crunchy vegetables, or as a spread on lettuce, pita or tortillas.

Preparation time: 15 minutes
Yields: 2 cups

Preparation Hints
This can be made spicier by adding onions and more garlic cloves to the recipe. To thin this into a dressing, add more water to the tahini. For a smoother sauces, put it through a blender.

Simply Salsa

Often salsa in a restaurant can taste as though it comes from a bottle. This recipe is the freshest, tastiest salsa ever. The secret ingredient is tomatillos. They look like little wrapped up green tomatoes. I enjoy eating the salsa over raw corn fresh off the cob. I take the corn kernels off the cob, flash them in a food processor. Then I warm them on the electric skillet, season with a tad of oil and spices and add the salsa. This is one of my favorite meals.

5 - 7 tomatoes

2 green onions

3 - 5 tomatillos

1 garlic clove (optional)

1/4 - 1/2 cup fresh cilantro

1 tsp chili

1 lime

Bragg's liquid aminos

Machine Instructions
Put the open blank screen over the twin gears. Then attach the pulp discharge casing without the outlet adjusting knob. Place a large enough bowl to catch any droppings from both the blank opening and the pulp discharge outlet.

Preparation and Serving Instructions
1. Alternate putting the tomatoes, green onions, tomatillos and garlic through the machine and into a bowl.
2. Stir the mixture, spicing with chili, lime juice and Bragg's to taste.
3. Stir in finely diced cilantro and serve. Or, chill and serve as a dip, top of tostadas, potatoes, or noodles.

Preparation time: 10 minutes
Yields: 3 cups

Preparation Hints
If you want a chunkier salsa, add two additional tomatoes and finely dice them into the sauce.

Southwestern Guacamole

First let us set the record straight, avocado has no cholesterol. It is rich in essential oils, and it is 70% water, quite an unusual combination. This fat is more easily digested, being unsaturated. Magnificent raw, in salads or in a dip, it also makes a terrific facial.

2 avocados

6 – 8 dried tomatoes

2 green onions

1 garlic clove (optional)

1 lemon

Bragg's liquid aminos

Machine Instructions for making the sauce
Put the open blank screen over the twin gears. Then attach the pulp discharge casing without the outlet adjusting knob. Place a large enough bowl to catch any droppings from both the blank opening and the pulp discharge outlet.

Preparation and Serving Instructions
1. Alternate putting the avocado, dried tomatoes, green onions and garlic (optional) through the machine and into a bowl.
2. Stir the mixture, spicing with lemon juice and Bragg's to taste.
3. Serve fresh or chill. Best served as a dip, or on top of tostadas, potatoes or salads.

Preparation time: 10 minutes
Yields: 2 Cups

Preparation Hints
If you want to make a dressing from this dip, add fresh tomatoes and put through the machine. If you want a chunkier dip, take an additional avocado and mash it gently with a fork into the final mixture.

That's a My Tomato Sauce

Tomatoes turn acidic when they are cooked and aggravate many health problems, especially arthritis. By not cooking the tomatoes, this easy-to-digest sauce will enhance your loaf, potato, noodle, vegetable or salad dishes.

4 tomatoes

1/2 – 1 cup dried tomatoes

1 – 2 garlic cloves

2 green onions

1 lime or lemon

Bragg's liquid amino

1 red or yellow bell pepper

1/2 cup fresh parsley

Machine Instructions

Put the open blank screen over the twin gears. Then attach the pulp discharge casing on without the outlet adjusting knob. Place a large enough bowl to catch any droppings from both the blank opening and the pulp discharge outlet.

Preparation and Serving Instructions

1. Alternate putting the fresh and dried tomatoes, garlic and green onions through the machine and into a bowl.
2. Stir the mixture spicing with lime or lemon juice, and Bragg's to taste.
3. Stir in finely diced bell pepper and parsley.
4. Serve as a sauce on top of nut loaves, vegetables, potatoes or noodles.

Preparation time: 20 minutes
Yields: 2 cups

Preparation Hints

Texture can be chunky or smooth. It is a matter of choice. If you desire a chunkier sauce, add a finely diced tomato and some finely diced onions.

Chapter IX

What's for Supper? Casseroles, Croquettes, Loaves, Patties, Patés and Rolls

The beauty of the Green Power machine is that whether you want to eat grains, nuts or vegetables, they can be made into a variety of wonderful recipes. These dishes can be eaten raw or warmed in a skillet or dehydrator at 105°F, warmed by the sun or chilled in the refrigerator. Whichever way you prefer, you will have a variety of dishes for lunch or dinner.

..onut Pecan Patty

..c pickle is a popular East Indian spice. If you like your food spicy, you will love this dish. I first made this with Johnny Lynch on my television show. He loves spicy food and this recipe reflects a toned down version of his recipe.

1-1/2 cup barley (soaked 4 – 6 hours, rinsed)

1 fresh coconut

(or 1 cup dehydrated unsweetened coconut flakes)

1-1/2 cup fresh pecans

1/2 – 1 tsp garlic pickle

Machine Instructions

Put the closed blank screen over the twin gears. Then attach the pulp discharge casing without the outlet adjusting knob. Place a bowl to catch the droppings from the outlet.

Preparation and Serving Instructions

1. Soak barley 4 – 6 hours, and rinse.
2. First put the barley, then the fresh or dehydrated coconut and finally the pecans through the machine and into a bowl.
3. Stir the mixture spicing with garlic pickle or Indian curry to taste.
4. Form patties 1/2-inch thick, 2 – 3-inches in diameter.
5. Serve with tomato or cucumber slices, sprouts, salad greens or veggie chips.

Soaking time: 4 – 6 hours
Preparation time: 15 minutes
Yields: 6 – 8 patties

Preparation Hints

Opening a fresh coconut is a neat experience. One of the simplest ways is to insert an ice pick into the soft spot on the top, and drain out the coconut milk. Once drained, a hammer will then shatter the shell. Using a butter knife, separate the meat from the shell. Eating fresh coconut is quite a treat. If you cannot find garlic pickle in an Indian store, you could use a curry spice and granulated garlic mix.

Southwestern Patty

This recipe is a favorite when you want to serve a patty that looks like meat but does not have any of the problems associated with eating meat, like hormones or drugs fed to the animals. Sunflower seeds and carrots are full of protein (6 grams per tablespoon) and calcium.

1 cup sunflower seeds

(soaked 8 – 12 hours, rinsed)

3 – 4 carrots

1 beet

1 cup parsley, finely chopped

vege-sal

Machine Instructions

Put the closed blank screen over the twin gears. Then attach the pulp discharge casing without the outlet adjusting knob and place a bowl to catch the droppings from the outlet.

Preparation and Serving Instructions

1. Soak sunflower seeds 8 – 12 hours, and rinse.
2. Alternate putting the sunflower seeds, carrots and beets through the machine and into a bowl.
3. Stir the finely diced parsley into the mixture, spicing with vege-sal to taste.
4. Form into patties 1/2-inch thick by 2 – 3 inches round.
5. Warm in the dehydrator at 105°F and serve with tomato or cucumber slices, lettuce, sprouts and favorite topping. Great with a salad or soup.

Soaking time: 8 – 12 hours
Preparation time: 15 minutes
Yields: 6 – 10 patties

Preparation Hints

If you want this to be a drier mixture, let the sunflower seeds dry out for a while on a tray or other flat surface. Dehydrating sunflower seeds both enhances the flavor and makes them firmer to eat.

Barley Warmed Casserole

This dish is unbelievable warmed in an electric skillet, kept on low and simmered just enough for the flavors to blend into a delightfully rich, satisfying and crunchy dish.

2 cups barley (soaked for 6 - 8 hours, rinsed)

1 cup oats (soaked for 4 - 6 hours, rinsed)

4 – 6 fresh tomatoes

1/2 cup dried tomatoes

1/2 cup fresh parsley

vege-sal

Machine Instructions
Put the open blank screen over the twin gears. Then attach the pulp discharge casing without the outlet adjusting knob. Place a large enough bowl to catch any droppings from both the blank opening and the pulp discharge outlet.

Preparation and Serving Instructions
1. First soak and rinse the barley and oats.
2. Put the soaked barley through the machine.
3. Then alternate putting the fresh and dried tomatoes through the machine and into a bowl.
4. Put the tomato sauce into an electric skillet, on warm, and stir the ground barley and whole oats into the sauce, simmering together until warm.
5. Stir in finely diced parsley, spicing with vege-sal to taste.
6. Serve warm.

Soaking time: 6 – 8 hours
Preparation time: 20 minutes
Yields: 4 – 6 servings

Preparation Hints
The barley can be left whole, but the difference in texture between the ground barley and whole oats can be very pleasing.

Blanch, My Almond Paté

Almonds are such a filling and nutritious nut. The beauty of raw foods is that the enzyme that helps digests the nut, lipase, is in the nut. Nature does know how to perfectly package her foods.

2 cups almonds, soaked and blanched (skinned)
3 carrots
1 garlic clove
1 lemon
1/4 cup fresh parsley
6 celery stalks
2 wedge-shaped slices of purple cabbage (to make chips for dipping)
1 unwaxed cucumber

Machine Instructions

Put the closed blank screen over the twin gears. Then attach the pulp discharge casing without the outlet adjusting knob. Place a bowl to catch the droppings from the outlet.

Preparation and Serving Instructions

1. Soak almonds 8 – 12 hours, rinse and blanch. Blanching is done by pouring hot water over the almonds immediately after rinsing. The skins should just pop off. If they do not, add more boiling water and let them soak longer.
2. Alternate putting the blanched almonds, carrots, garlic and celery stalks through the machine and into a bowl.
3. Stir the mixture spicing with lemon juice to taste and form the paté into a pyramid or other fun shape.
4. Garnish the paté with finely diced parsley and surround with purple cabbage and sliced celery and cucumber.

Soaking time: 8 – 12 hours
Blanching time: 20 – 30 minutes
Preparation time: 15 minutes
Yields: 6 – 8 servings

Preparation Hints

Creating a fun-shaped paté and adding an abundance of colorful vegetable sticks makes this tasty dish a hit at any celebration.

Brightly Beet-Carrot Paté

A delightfully easy spread to prepare with the handy Green Power machine as your kitchen sidekick. Dr. Cousens introduced me to this recipe at one of his workshops.

4 – 6 carrots

1/2 cup beets

1 cup sunflower seeds
(soaked 6 – 8 hours, rinsed)

2 red or yellow bell peppers

4 fresh tomatoes

1 lime, or raw apple cider vinegar

cayenne and/or cumin

Machine Instructions
Put the closed blank screen over the twin gears. Then attach the pulp discharge casing without the outlet adjusting knob. Place a bowl to catch the droppings from the outlet.

Preparation and Serving Instructions
1. Soak sunflower seeds 8 – 12 hours, rinse .
2. Alternate putting the carrots, beets and sunflower seeds through the machine and into a bowl.
3. Stir the mixture adding finely diced bell peppers and tomatoes, spicing with lime juice or raw apple cider and cayenne and/or cumin to taste.
4. Form the paté loaf.
5. Serve with greens, crackers or veggie chips.

Soaking time: 8 – 12 hours
Preparation time: 15 minutes
Yields: 6 – 8 servings

Preparation Hints
This colorful and tasty dish is best served after it sits for about 30 minutes. The time gives the flavors a chance to mingle with each other.

Celebration Loaf

My friend Adia first showed me her version of this loaf on my television show. She said that whenever she made this loaf for a party, she always went home with a clean plate. I have had the same experience with my version. A definite winner!

1 cup sunflower seeds (soaked 8 – 12 hours, rinsed)

1 cup almonds (soaked 8 – 12 hours, rinsed)

1 garlic clove

2 – 3 carrots

2 celery stalks

1/2 red or yellow onion

2 bell peppers (1 red, 1 yellow)

1 cup parsley, finely chopped

Bragg's or Dr. Jensen's Quick Sip

Machine Instructions
Put the closed blank screen over the twin gears. Then attach the pulp discharge casing on without the outlet adjusting knob. Place a bowl to catch the droppings from the outlet and you are ready to prepare a cholesterol-free loaf.

Preparation and Serving Instructions
1. Soak sunflower seeds and almonds separately for 8 – 12 hours, and rinse.
2. Alternate putting the sunflower seeds, almonds, garlic and carrots through the machine and into a bowl.
3. Stir the mixture adding finely diced celery, onion, bell peppers and parsley, spicing with Bragg's or Dr. Jensen's Quick Sip to taste.
4. Form the paté into one or two loaves, garnishing with parsley.
5. Warm in a dehydrator at 105°F, or put into a sunny window sill and let warm. Great served with a salad, soup or on its own.

Soaking time: 8 – 12 hours
Preparation time: 15 minutes
Yields: 1 large loaf or 2 smaller ones, 6 – 8 servings

Preparation Hints
I basted this loaf with Such a Sweet Sauce, and then dehydrated it until it was warm all the way through, about 4 – 6 hours. Try it served plain or with That's a My Tomato Sauce.

Beyond Tuna Stuffing

This unique recipe uses the pulp left over from juicing carrots. It uses the Creamy Thousand Island Dressing recipe to make a stuffing, a loaf or patties. Nicknamed Beyond Gabriel, after Dr. Gabriel Cousens, this is a favorite at the Tree of Life Rejuvenation Center.

3 cups of carrot pulp

2 bell peppers (1 red and 1 yellow)

1/2 red onion

2 celery stalks

1 cup fresh parsley

1-1/2 cup of Creamy Thousand Island Dressing

(from Chapter IX – save 1/2 cup of dressing for topping)

1 lemon

2 - 4 tsp Jensen's veggie broth

Machine Instructions

For this recipe you will need freshly juiced carrot pulp. So, set your Green Power machine for juicing. Put the fine screen over the twin gears. Then attach the pulp discharge casing with the outlet adjusting knob in place, loosening the knob as you juice to allow the pulp to come out. Place the pitcher under the juice outlet and a bowl under the pulp discharge outlet.

Preparation and Serving Instructions

1. Finely dice the bell peppers, red onion, celery and fresh parsley.
2. In a large bowl stir the finely diced ingredients with the carrot pulp and 1 cup of the Creamy Thousand Island Dressing.
3. Spice with lemon juice and Jensen's veggie broth to taste.
4. Stuff into a scooped out tomato, celery stick or bell pepper. Serve with sprouts and salad greens and a spoonful of dressing.

Soaking time: 4 - 6 hours
Preparation time: 15 minutes
Yields: 6 - 8 patties

Preparation Hints

The key to the taste of this recipe is the finely diced ingredients which give texture to the carrot pulp. Also, the amount of dressing desired is personal preference.

Stuffed Grape Leaves Roll

This raw version of stuffed grape leaves is a winner. As an appetizer or main dish, it gets rave reviews. Usually the leaves are stuffed with rice or meat, but in this recipe, the oats and avocado make a rich and creamy filling that is both healthy and satisfying.

1 jar grape leaves

2 cups oat groats (soaked 4 - 8 hours, rinsed)

1 avocado

2 green onion

2 celery stalks

1 unwaxed cucumber

Machine Instructions

Put the closed blank screen over the twin gears. Then attach the pulp discharge casing without the outlet adjusting knob and place a bowl to catch the droppings from the outlet.

Preparation and Serving Instructions

1. Soak the oat groats for 4 – 8 hours, and rinse.
2. To make the stuffing dip, alternate putting half the oat groats, avocado, green onion, celery and half the cucumber through the machine and into a bowl.
3. Rinse the grape leaves, cut off stem and put 1 – 2 teaspoons of the stuffing dip on the edge closest to you, folding the sides in, and roll closed.
4. Serve on a platter, with the remaining half of the cucumber sliced thin as a garnish. This is delicious with a tahini dip (sesame butter).

Soaking time: 4 - 8 hours
Preparation time: 20 minutes
Yields: 10 - 15 rolls

Preparation Hints

I like the stuffing dip without any additional spicing. But, if you want it more tart, add lemon or lime juice. If you want a saltier taste, add Bragg's liquid aminos or tamari soy sauce.

Pecan Paté

Stuffed into pepper boats, this dish is both lovely to look at and deceptively simple to make. Let your guests guess the ingredients. The secret ingredient is the poultry spice. Ed Douglas has a genius for spicing that I do appreciate. I think you will enjoy it too.

2 cups fresh pecans

1/2 – 1 red onion

1 tsp poultry spice

Bragg's liquid aminos

1 lemon

2 bell peppers (red or yellow or one of each)

parsley

Machine Instructions

Put the closed blank screen over the twin gears. Then attach the pulp discharge casing without the outlet adjusting knob. Place a bowl to catch the droppings from the outlets.

Preparation and Serving Instructions

1. Alternate putting the pecans and onion through the machine and into a bowl.
2. Stir the mixture, spicing with poultry spice, Bragg's and lemon juice to taste.
3. Stuff the paté into half a bell pepper, garnish with parsley.
4. Warm in a dehydrator at 105°F. Serve with a salad or soup.

Preparation time: 15 minutes
Yields: 4 stuffed pepper boats

Preparation Hints

If you want to make this paté thinner, add a bit of water to the mixture once it is blended through the machine. It can even be thinned enough to be a dip.

Curried Croquettes

This is another recipe I have made with the terrific culinary advice of Johnny Lynch. He helped me understand how to use spices to make a good recipe better. The Indian Curry Paste is the best I have found, and I have included where to find it in the Resources section.

2 cups wheat berries, white spring wheat (soaked and sprouted)

2 cups raw cashews

spice options: 1 – 2 tsp Instant Indian Curry Paste or

2 tsp tomato pickle and 2 tsp Mexican seasoning

Machine Instructions

Put the closed blank screen over the twin gears. Then attach the pulp discharge casing without the outlet adjusting knob. Place a bowl to catch the droppings from the outlets.

Preparation and Serving Instructions

1. Soak wheat 8 – 12 hours, rinse and let sprout for 8 – 12 hours, rinsing once or twice as needed.
2. Alternate putting the wheat and cashews through the machine and into a bowl.
3. Stir the mixture spicing with Instant India Curry or tomato pickle and Mexican seasoning to taste.
4. Form croquettes into 1/2-inch thick, 2 – 3-inches mini-loaf shapes.
5. Serve with tomato or cucumber slices, sprouts, salad greens or veggie chips.

Soaking time: 8 – 12 hours
Sprouting time 8 – 12 hours
Preparation time: 15 minutes
Yields: 8 – 12 croquettes

Preparation Hints

Tomato pickle is an East Indian spice. Mexican seasoning is a mixture found in most natural food markets. But, the Instant India Curry Paste really makes this dish special. It is worth the effort to find it in your area or call the distributor.

Nutty Nut Patty

My friend Adia showed me a version of this recipe on my television show. It is delicious even in its simplest form. With the beet included, it almost looks like meat. To tell or not to tell, that is the question?

1 cup sunflower seeds (soaked 8 – 12 hours, rinsed)

1 cup almonds (soaked 8 – 12 hours, rinsed)

3 carrots

1 garlic clove

1 beet

2 celery stalks

1/2 red or yellow onion

1/2 cup fresh parsley

Bragg's liquid aminos or

Dr. Bronner's mineral powder

Machine Instructions

Put the closed blank screen over the twin gears. Then attach the pulp discharge casing without the outlet adjusting knob. Place a bowl to catch the droppings from the outlets.

Preparation and Serving Instructions

1. Soak sunflower seeds and almonds separately for 8 – 12 hours and rinse.
2. Alternate putting the sunflower seeds, almonds, carrots, garlic, and beet through the machine and into a bowl.
3. Stir the mixture adding finely diced celery, onion, bell peppers and parsley, spicing with Bragg's or Dr. Bronner's mineral powder to taste.

4. Form into patties, 1/2-inch thick by 2 – 3-inches round.
5. Warm in the dehydrator at 105°F until warm, or put in a sunny window sill and let warm. Great with tomato or cucumber slices, lettuce, sprouts and toppings of your choice.

Soaking time: 8 – 12 hours
Preparation time: 15 minutes
Yields: 6 – 10 patties

Preparation Hints

This is tasty served with Such a Sweet Sauce or formed into loaves and served with soup or salad.

Sunny Broccoli-Carrot Paté

This recipe was created at a workshop offered by Dr. Gabriel Cousens, and I enjoy making it for friends, especially at holiday time. I prepared it for one of my TV shows, called Christmas Crunch.

1-1/2 cup pumpkin seeds (soaked 8 - 12 hours, rinsed)

2 – 4 carrots

1 cup broccoli

1/4 cup basil

1 Tbsp fresh ginger

2 celery stalks

1 – 2 tsp red miso

1 lemon or raw apple cider vinegar

Machine Instructions
Put the closed blank screen over the twin gears. Then attach the pulp discharge casing without the outlet adjusting knob and place a bowl to catch the droppings from the outlets.

Preparation and Serving Instructions
1. Soak the pumpkin seeds for 8 – 12 hours, and rinse.
2. Alternate putting the pumpkin seeds, carrots, broccoli (save a few flowerettes for garnishing), basil (save a few leaves for garnishing), ginger and a celery stalk through the machine and into a bowl.
3. Stir the mixture adding finely chopped celery, spicing with red miso and lemon juice or raw apple cider vinegar to taste.
4. Mold into a fun shape, garnish with broccoli flowerettes and basil leaves, and serve over salad greens, crackers or veggie chips.

Soaking time: 8 – 12 hours
Preparation time: 25 minutes
Yields: 4 – 6 servings

Preparation Hints
There are many types of miso. I prefer the flavor of red miso, but you can use other flavors. I take the skin off the broccoli stalk and use it with the flowerettes. To get the flowerettes through the machine with ease, put the flowered side down and use part of a carrot to push it through the machine. This paté is tasty formed into a patty, dehydrated for 4 – 6 hours, and served warm with all trimmings - tomato, cucumber, lettuce, sprouts and your favorite dressing on top.

Whata Walnut Loaf

This is a rich nutty loaf, spiced like a barbequed dish. Liquid Smoke is found in most markets in the spice section and garlic pickle can be found in East Indian food markets. Johnny Lynch was the inspiration for this dish. He likes his food hot and spicy. You can modify the spices to suit your tastes.

1-1/2 cups raw walnuts

1-1/2 cups raw pine nuts

1 cup fresh parsley

1/2 jicama

2 red or yellow bell peppers

Spice options

1 tsp fresh dill

1/4 tsp Liquid Smoke

1 tsp garlic pickle

2 tsp Tomato Delight

Machine Instructions

Put the open blank screen over the twin gears. Then attach the pulp discharge casing without the outlet adjusting knob and place a large enough bowl to catch any droppings from both the blank opening and the outlets.

Preparation and Serving Instructions

1. Process each ingredient separately. First, put the walnuts, then the pine nuts through the machine and into a bowl.
2. Stir the mixture adding 1/4 finely diced jicama and parsley, spicing with dill, Liquid Smoke, garlic pickle and Tomato Delight to taste.
3. Form into a loaf, surrounded by jicama and bell pepper slices.
4. Warm in the dehydrator at 105°F. Serve with soup or salad.

Preparation time: 15 minutes
Yields: 1 loaf, 6 – 8 servings

Preparation Hints

This is a rich dish, and needs a lot of water-rich foods served with it. Fresh coconut could be added. If so, put through the machine separately during step one.

Up Beet Rolls

Beet greens are tasty and make a colorful meal or appetizer when rolled with stuffing. This dish is upbeat and full of flavors. I love to serve trays of these before supper. I call these paw foods because you can eat them with your hands.

beet greens

Stuffing

2 – 3 beets
1 daikon
2 carrots

Sauce

2 avocados
2 green onions
1/2 cup cilantro
1 lemon
Bragg's liquid aminos

Machine Instructions (For making the sauce)
Put the closed blank screen over the twin gears. Then attach the pulp discharge casing without the outlet adjusting knob and place a bowl to catch the droppings from the outlet.

Preparation and Serving Instructions

1. Fill a 9-inch glass pie plate with hot water and dip each beet green into the hot water for a moment. Remove when it is soft and lie flat on a plate.
2. In separate bowls, finely grate the beets, daikon and carrots.
3. To make the topping sauce, alternate putting the avocado, green onion and cilantro through the machine and into a bowl, spicing with lemon juice and Bragg's to taste.
4. In each beet leaf put a small line of grated beets, daikon and carrots next to each other, and pour the sauce on top. Gently roll the leaf closed.
5. Serve on a platter, with a bowl of the sauce in the middle.

Preparation time: 20 minutes
Yields: 15 – 20 rolls

Preparation Hints
Pick the largest beet greens you can find. They need to be large and soft enough to roll. A toothpick can help keep them closed, and make them easier to pick up. Otherwise make sure the last end is tucked down, resting on the plate to keep them gently closed. The trick is putting a small amount in for stuffing. The sauce can be laced on top for visual appeal, but this is a bit messier to eat with your hands.

Sprouted Nori Rolls

Nori, thin black sheets of seaweed often used for sushi, is a rich source of calcium and iodine. This dish can be served as an appetizer or as a meal on its own.

2 cups almonds (soaked 8 – 12 hours, rinsed)

1 cup sunflower seeds (soaked 8 – 12 hours, rinsed)

1 Tbsp fresh ginger

1/2 tsp sesame oil

1 lemon

Bragg's liquid aminos

6 – 10 nori sheets

3 cups alfalfa or clover sprouts

1 carrot (cut into long thin peeled sticks)

1 avocado (cut into long thin strips)

1 cucumber (cut into long thin strips)

1 broccoli stalk (the flowerettes will be used)

Machine Instructions
Put the closed blank screen over the twin gears. Then attach the pulp discharge casing without the outlet adjusting knob and place a bowl to catch the droppings from the outlets.

Preparation and Serving Instructions
1. Soak sunflower seeds and almonds separately for 8 – 12 hours, and rinse.
2. Alternate putting the sunflower seeds, almonds and fresh ginger through the machine and into a bowl.
3. Stir the stuffing mixture adding sesame oil and spicing with lemon juice and Bragg's to taste.
4. Spread sprouts across nori sheet, near the edge closest to you. Next, spread stuffing mixture on top across sprouts, adding a thin strip of carrot, avocado and cucumber. Cover with sprouts and roll nori tightly, wetting the far edge of nori to seal it shut.
5. With a sharp knife, slice rolls 1 – 2-inches thick and put a broccoli flowerette in one end of each section, serve immediately. Great served with miso soup or salad.

Soaking time: 8 – 12 hours
Preparation time: 20 minutes
Yields: 6 – 10 rolls

Preparation Hints
Make sure that you put the nori on a perfectly dry surface, as it softens when moistened. Keeping the sprouts evenly distributed makes it easier to roll. I find that when I gently pull the nori back toward me and roll slowly, it stays tight and firm. If you are one of those cooks who wants to use every ingredient, the broccoli stalk can be used inside the nori roll. Peel the outer layer and cut the broccoli stalk into long thin strips, similar to the carrots. The stalk is delightfully moist and tasty.

Chapter X

On the Grainy Side: Crackers, Breads, Pastries and Porridges

Working with grains and the Green Power machine is a whole new effortless world for me. I found a food processor and blender cumbersome, and often unevenly blended grains. Getting them out of the machines was also a chore which resulted in cut fingers from the sharp blades. With the Green Power machine, the twin gears do not cut fingers. And, if I soak the parts in warm water for a while, the clean up is a breeze. I have tried various ways of preparing the grains. If I use the open blank on the machine, the grains come out less ground. If you want a chewier grain dish use this technique. Otherwise, for most of the grains I prefer a finer grind. For this purpose, I use the closed blank. If I want them to come out prerolled, in a bread stick form, I use the rice cake attachment instead of the outlet adjusting knob. This method

has saved me hours of time as the dough was already prerolled. So, whether you make pretzels, twists or other decorative breads, enjoy the creative process.

A word about dehydrators. The people at Health Force Regeneration Systems introduced me to the Excalibur dehydrator and I am so thankful. I bought a square, nine drawer model. This dehydrator has many advantages over the round models. First of all, the temperature can be adjusted. Second, the air blows from the back to the front evenly, not from bottom to top, making the bottom tray drier than the others. Third, there is the possibility of modifying the space between the trays. Not only can it accommodate cracker and cookie dough, but also it can also fit spring molds and pie plates to warm up sauces or other dishes.

There are reusable teflex sheets that can be purchased and used for the trays when liquid substances are dehydrated, like the cracker mixture or dried fruit rolls. There are special wax paper sheets available which I have used on the road. Plain wax paper can shed on the food, making it unnecessarily waxy.

While I bought a timer for my machine, now some come with a built-in timer. This allows me to turn on and off the machine, whether I am home or not. If your machine does not have a timer built-in, buy one. It is a handy and inexpensive investment available at most any hardware store. Also, the motor on the dehydrator is noisy. For this reason, I keep mine in a separate room.

If you do not have a dehydrator, I have tried warming some of the dishes in the sun, or on a counter, which works for the dryer doughs. For a wetter dough, having warm air blow continually across it helps it dry evenly. The oven can be experimented with, but needs careful monitoring so the dishes do not get too hot. For one dish, I let the oven warm up and then turned off the heat altogether. Then, I left the dish in the oven overnight and it did the trick. So until you decide it is a worthwhile investment to buy a dehydrator, experiment with what is at hand: your oven, a window sill or the counter.

Different climates create different dehydration times. Living near the ocean is a much moister environment than living inland. For this reason, I have put a range of times. You will need to check and find out what timing works best for your area, and how it changes during each season. You can soften food that has been overdehydrated by putting it into a plastic or glass container with fresh salad greens, covered by a paper towel. To avoid this hassle, check your dehydrating foods frequently so as not to overdry them.

The reason I use 105°F as the maximum temperature is to preserve as many enzymes as possible. Amino acids seem to the be the most delicate, and I was informed by several sources that they start to be destroyed around 110°F. So to play it safe, go five degrees less and all the enzymes will remain intact.

As for the ingredients in this section, find grains that you enjoy. Our local natural food store carries a wide selection of organic grains. I continue to experiment with some new ones. Rye, kamut, wheat and spelt are some of the heavier grains. Barley and oats tend to be lighter. When you are making crackers, spice less to start with, and add more to taste. A potato masher stirs the dough best, although a fork will do the job with a bit more elbow grease. The thinner the cracker, the faster it dries and the crisper it will be. For a chewier cracker, make them thicker. The more fresh ingredients you add, the thinner the dough. Have fun cutting the crackers with cookie cutters or use the drop method, spooning the dough on to the trays in a more irregular pattern. (Spreading them out on the tray or teflex sheets gives a more homemade look. Both a spatula and a pizza cutter work well for scoring the cracker sheets.)

Breads are another story. They are thicker and take longer to dry. But both breads and crackers have the possibility to be sweet or salty. Anise seed, figs, raisins, dates, bananas, cinnamon, nutmeg, allspice, vanilla or Chinese 5 spice are some of the choices for making a sweet cracker or bread. For a saltier taste, celery, peppers, parsley, basil, dill, cilantro, onions, garlic, cumin seed, dill seed, caraway seed or fennel seed and lemon or lime juice or rind can be added. See what inspires you and come up with your own recipes.

Different breads can be made by making loafs, twisted bread sticks, pretzels or other creative shapes. Muffins or smaller loafs can be made. I like to use a 1/2 measuring cup to scoop out the dough for more uniform amounts. Be creative with the following recipes. Play with your food, and see what happens.

Beets Me Crackers

Kamut is a large grain, with a gluten content similar to wheat, but without the allergic problems often associated with wheat. The bright red color make this a favorite during the holidays.

2 cups kamut (soaked 8 – 12 hours, sprouted 12 – 24 hours)

1/2 beet

1 red pepper

6 cherry tomatoes or 2 regular tomatoes

2 – 3 tsp vege-sal

1 tsp granulated garlic

Machine Instructions
Put the closed blank screen over the twin gears. Then attach the pulp discharge casing without the outlet adjusting knob. Place a large enough bowl to catch the droppings from the outlet.

Preparation and Serving Instructions
1. Soak kamut 8 – 12 hours, rinse and let sprout 12 – 24 hours, rinsing as needed.
2. Alternate putting the kamut, beet, red pepper and tomatoes through the machine and into a bowl.
3. Stir into the mixture the spices to taste, and spread the mixture out onto dehydrator trays, covered with teflex, or wax paper. Spread it 1/4-inch thick, in a rectangular shape, and cut it with a spatula into crackers 2-inch by 2-inch square or as you prefer.

4. Set the dehydrator at 105°F, and dehydrate until crisp, about 8 – 16 hours, depending on weather and climate. Check occasionally, rescore and turn over, taking off the teflex sheet (or wax paper) when the first half is done.
5. Serve warm or store in covered containers.

Soaking time: 8 – 12 hours
Sprouting time: 12 - 24 hours
Preparation time: 25 minutes
Dehydrating time: 8 - 16 hours
Yields: 20 – 30 crackers

Preparation Hints
Kamut is a hearty grain. To avoid the machine clogging, use a little at a time, letting the gears pull the grain in gradually. If you put too much in, push it through gently with the plunger, and slow down.

113

Barley Sticky Buns

Sweetened with raisins and currants, these cinnamoned creations are a fine morning treat.

2 cups barley (soaked 8 – 12 hours, rinsed)
1 cup organic raisins
1 cup organic currants
1 – 2 tsp cinnamon
1 – 2 thin slices of ginger

Machine Instructions
Put the closed blank screen over the twin gears and then attach the pulp discharge casing with the rice cake guide securely in place. Place a tray to catch the bread sticks dough from the outlet.

Preparation and Serving Instructions
1. Soak barley for 8 – 12 hours, rinse.
2. Alternate putting the barley and raisins through the machine and into a bowl.
3. Stir, spicing with the cinnamon to taste.
4. Catch the rolls as they leave the machine, form into round buns, pinch off and start again.
5. In a blender, mix the currants and ginger with enough water to make a thick paste. Baste the top of the buns and sprinkle with cinnamon.
6. Dehydrate on a tray at 105°F for 6 – 12 hours.
5. Serve warm or store in a plastic bag in the refrigerator. Tasty served with more of the warmed currant sauce.

Soaking time: 8 – 12 hours
Preparation time: 20 minutes
Dehydrating time: 6 – 16 hours
Yields: 8 – 16 buns

Preparation Hints
If you are working with a friend, one puts the barley and raisins through the machine, the other catches the dough, pinching off the length of dough needed to roll into a bun. If you are working alone, put a tray on a tall bowl, so that the dough will go onto the tray, pinch off the length you need and continue to move the tray until the process is done. At the end you will be able to roll up the buns. The currant sauce can be warmed in a glass pie plate in the dehydrator.

Mexi-Flax Crackers

These crackers were a favorite at Dr. Cousens' center. They were usually gone within two days of making them.

2 cups flax seeds
(soaked 2 – 8 hours, no rinsing necessary)
2 fresh tomatoes
1/2 cup dried tomatoes
1 red bell pepper
1 – 3 tsp Mexican seasoning

Machine Instructions
Put the open blank screen over the twin gears. Then attach the pulp discharge casing without the outlet adjusting knob. Place a large enough bowl to catch the droppings from the outlet.

Instructions
1. Soak the flax seeds 2 – 8 hours, no rinsing is necessary.
2. Alternate putting the tomatoes and bell pepper through the machine and into a bowl.
3. Stir the soaked flax seeds into the mixture, spicing to taste. Spread the mixture out onto dehydrator trays, covered with teflex, or wax paper. Spread it 1/4-inch thick, in a rectangular shape, and 'score' it with a spatula into crackers 2 by 2-inches or any dimensions you prefer.
4. Set the dehydrator at 105°F and dehydrate until crisp, about 8 – 16 hours, depending on weather and climate. Check occasionally, rescore and turn over, taking off the teflex sheet (or wax paper) when the first half is done.
5. Serve warm or store in covered containers.

Soaking time: 2 – 8 hours
Preparation time: 25 minutes
Dehydrating time: 8 – 16 hours
Yields: 20 – 30 crackers

Preparation Hints
The thicker you spread the cracker mixture, the longer it will be to dehydrate them. (The thicker crackers are chewier.) Also, thinner crackers tend to be crisper.

Lean Green Protein Crackers

This high protein, calcium rich cracker is a winner. The Green Power machine makes this cracker a pleasure to prepare. The caraway and dill make it taste like a rye cracker.

2 cups sunflower seeds
(soaked 8 – 12 hours, rinse)

1/2 cup kamut
(soaked 8 – 12 hours, sprouted 12 – 24 hours)

2 celery stalks

1/4 cup fresh parsley

1/4 cup fresh dill weed

1 tsp ground caraway seeds

vege-sal

Machine Instructions
Put the closed blank screen over the twin gears. Then attach the pulp discharge casing without the outlet adjusting knob. Place a large enough bowl to catch the droppings from the outlet.

Preparation and Serving Instructions
1. Soak the kamut 8 – 12 hours, rinse and let sprout 12 – 24 hours (while the sunflower seeds are soaking), rinsing as needed. Soak the sunflower seeds 8 – 12 hours before needed, rinse.
2. Alternate putting the sunflower seeds, kamut and celery through the machine into a bowl.
3. Stir into the mixture finely diced parsley and dill, spicing to taste with the caraway seeds and vege-sal. Spread the mixture out onto dehydrator trays, covered with teflex, or wax paper so the dough will not drip through the trays. Spread it 1/4-inch thick, in a rectangular shape, and cut it with a spatula into crackers 2 by 2-inches or any dimensions you prefer.

4. Set the dehydrator at 105°F, and dehydrate until crisp, about 8 – 16 hours, depending on weather and climate. Check occasionally, rescore and turn over, taking off the teflex sheet (or wax paper) when the first half is done.
5. Serve warm or store in covered containers.

Soaking time: 8 – 12 hours
Sprouting time: 12 – 24 hours
Preparation time: 25 minutes
Dehydrating time: 8 – 16 hours
Yields: 20 – 30 crackers

Preparation Hints
The fresh parsley and dill make this cracker rich in chlorophyll, and the parsley is rich in iron. Make sure you chop the ingredients very fine so there are no chunks in your crackers.

116

Barley Warmed Bread

4 cups barley
(soaked 8 – 12 hours, rinsed)

2 cups sunflower seeds
(soaked 8 – 12 hours, rinsed)

2 – 3 tsp ground cumin

2 – 3 tsp ground dill seed

2 – 3 tsp vege-sal, or Spike

2 Tbsp fresh dill weed

Machine Instructions

Put the closed blank screen over the twin gears. Then attach the pulp discharge casing with the rice cake guide securely in place. Place a bowl to catch the droppings from the outlet.

Preparation and Serving Instructions

1. Soak barley and the sunflower seeds separately for 8 – 12 hours, rinse.
2. Alternate putting the barley and sunflower seeds through the machine and into a bowl.
3. Stir the mixture, spicing to taste with cumin, dill seeds and vege-sal.
4. Form into two long narrow loaves, not more than 1 – 1-1/2-inches thick, garnishing with the fresh dill. Let dry in the sun 6 – 10 hours, or dehydrate at 105°F for 10 – 16 hours.
5. Serve warm or store in a plastic bag in the refrigerator. Lovely served with soup or salad, or with vegetable garnishes on top.

Soaking time: 8 – 12 hours
Preparation time: 20 minutes
Dehydrating time: 6 – 16 hours
Yields: 2 loaves

Italian Bread Sticks

I have always loved garlic bread and bread sticks. This recipe combines the best of both.

2 cups winter wheat berries
(soaked 8 – 12 hours, rinsed; sprouted 12 – 24 hours)
1/4 cup fresh finely diced basil
1/2 cup fresh finely diced parsley
2 cloves minced garlic
2 – 3 tsp Onion Magic
2 – 3 tsp vege-sal

Machine Instructions
Put the closed blank screen over the twin gears and then attach the pulp discharge casing with the rice cake guide securely in place. Put a tray to catch the bread sticks dough from the outlet.

Preparation and Serving Instructions
1. Soak the soft winter wheat for 8 – 12 hours, rinse, and let sprout for 12 – 24 hours, until a small tail emerges, rinsing as necessary.
2. Stir all the ingredients together in a bowl, and slowly spoon the mixture into the machine catching the bread sticks on a dehydrator tray, pinching off at the desired length.
3. Let dry in the sun 6 – 10 hours or dehydrate at 105°F for 4 – 8 hours.
4. Serve warm or store in a plastic bag in the refrigerator. Lovely served with soup, salad or your favorite dip.

Soaking time: 8 – 12 hours
Sprouting time: 12 – 24 hours
Preparation time: 20 minutes
Dehydrating time: 4 – 8 hours
Yields: many bread sticks

Preparation Hints
This process works well with two people, one to feed the machine, the other to catch the bread sticks, pinching each one off at the desired length. These take hardly any time at all to dry, so check them regularly.

119

Barley Spiced Crackers

The beauty of these crackers is that the vitamin B is kept intact by not cooking the grain. Pearl barley is what most people can find in their local natural food store. Barley is an easier grain to work with because it can be soaked and used on the same day.

2 cups barley (soak 6 – 8 hours, rinse)

1 cup sunflower seeds (soak 8 – 12 hours, rinse)

1 green pepper

1 – 2 tsp onion flakes

1/2 – 1 tsp ground cumin seed

1/2 – 1 tsp ground dill seed

2 – 3 tsp vege-sal or other salty seasoning

Machine Instructions

Put the closed blank screen over the twin gears. Then attach the pulp discharge casing without the outlet adjusting knob. Place a large enough bowl to catch the droppings from the outlet.

Preparation and Serving Instructions

1. Soak the sunflower seeds 8 – 12 hours, rinse. Soak barley 6 – 8 hours, rinse.
2. Alternate putting the barley, sunflower seeds and green pepper through the machine and into a bowl.
3. Stir into the mixture the spices to taste, and spread the mixture out onto dehydrator trays, covered with teflex, or wax paper (so the dough will not drip through). Spread it 1/4-inch thick, in a rectangular shape, and cut it with a spatula into crackers 2 by 2-inches or any dimensions you prefer.
4. Set the dehydrator at 105°F, and dehydrate until crisp, about 8 – 16 hours, depending on weather and climate. Check occasionally (at 4 to 8 hours), rescore and turn over, taking off the teflex sheet (or wax paper) when the first half is done.
5. Serve warm or store in covered containers.

Soaking time: 8 – 12 hours
Preparation time: 25 minutes
Dehydrating time: 8 – 16 hours
Yields: 20 – 30 crackers

Preparation Hints

For a dryer cracker, let the barley sit on a tray after rinsing and let dry for an hour or so. I used green peppers to keep the color on the green side, but try red or yellow bell peppers as well. The spice tends to get stronger when a food is dehydrated, so use less rather than more, until you get a feel for how spicy you like your crackers. This dough tends to be rather thick. Sometimes, I like to make different shaped crackers with molds or cookie cutters. If you hand shape this dough, then the teflex sheet is not necessary.

Crispy Oat Crackers

Oat groats, the whole oat, make a lighter cracker, similar to barley. Plus, basil is such a delightful flavor; best when it is fresh.

2 cups oat groats (soak 4 – 6 hours, rinse)
1 cup pumpkin seeds (soak 4 – 6 hours, rinse)
1 green onion
8 basil leaves
1 garlic clove
2 – 3 tsp spike, or other salty seasoning

Machine Instructions

Put the closed blank screen over the twin gears. Then attach the pulp discharge casing without the outlet adjusting knob. Place a large enough bowl to catch the droppings from the outlet.

Instructions

1. Soak the oat groats and pumpkin seeds 4 – 6 hours, rinse.
2. Alternate putting the oats, pumpkin seeds, green onion, basil and garlic through the machine and into a bowl.
3. Stir into the mixture the spices to taste, and spread the mixture out onto dehydrator trays, covered with teflex, or wax paper. Spread it 1/4-inch thick, in a rectangular shape, and cut it with a spatula into crackers 2 by 2-inches or any dimensions you prefer.
4. Set the dehydrator at 105°F, and dehydrate until crisp, about 8 – 16 hours, depending on weather and climate. Check occasionally, rescore and turn over, taking off the teflex sheet (or wax paper) when the first half is done.
5. Serve warm or store in covered containers.

Soaking time: 4 – 6 hours
Preparation time: 25 minutes
Dehydrating time: 8 – 16 hours
Yields: 20 – 30 crackers

Preparation Hints

If you want a drier cracker, let the oats dry on a tray for an hour or so. Experiment with different types of basil and see how the flavor is affected.

Royal Porridge

Oatmeal is such a treat on a cold day. For a real treat, make a sweet almond milk, blending almonds and water with dates and banana in a blender and pour this over the porridge.

2 cups oat groats (soak 4 – 6 hours, rinse)
1/2 box fresh blueberries
1/2 box fresh strawberries
1 – 2 tsp cinnamon

Machine Instructions

Put the closed blank screen over the twin gears and then attach the pulp discharge casing without the outlet adjusting knob. Place a large enough bowl to catch the droppings from the outlet.

Preparation and Serving Instructions

1. Soak the oats 4 – 6 hours, rinse.
2. Alternate putting the oats, fresh blueberries and strawberries through the machine and into a bowl.
3. Stir into the mixture putting a bit of cinnamon on top.
4. Serve in a bowl, garnish with extra blueberries and strawberries.

Soaking time: 4 – 6 hours
Preparation time: 25 minutes
Yields: 2 – 4 servings

Preparation Hints

Tastes great mixed with almond milk, Amazake or Rice Dream (available in most natural food stores). Making the almond milk is simple. Soak the almonds overnight, rinse, and put a handful in the blender with a cup or so of water, sweetening with a few pitted dates and/or a banana.

Winter Porridge

Barley is a soft grain. When it is blended with soft, sweet fruits, delicately spiced and gently warmed, it is a cold winter morning's delight.

1 cup barley
(soak 4 – 6 hours, rinse)
1/2 cup sunflower seeds
(soak 8 – 12 hours, rinse)
4 – 6 pitted prunes
2 – 4 pitted dates

spice options: 1/2 – 1 tsp cinnamon,
nutmeg or Chinese 5 spice

Machine Instructions

Put the closed blank screen over the twin gears and then attach the pulp discharge casing without the outlet adjusting knob. Place a large enough bowl to catch the droppings from the outlet.

Preparation and Serving Instructions

1. Soak the sunflower seeds 8 – 12 hours, rinse. Soak the barley 4 – 6 hours, rinse.
2. In a bowl, mix the barley and sunflower seeds with your spice choice(s).
3. Alternate putting the spiced barley and sunflower mixture with the dried fruit through the machine and into a bowl.
4. For a warmed porridge, pour hot water over the mixture (start with 1/8 cup) and blend, warming and thinning to desired consistency.
5. Serve in a bowl.

Soaking time: 8 – 12 hours
Preparation time: 15 minutes
Yields: 2 – 4 servings

Preparation Hints

Keeping this mixture wet is the easiest way to make this porridge. It can be eaten as is, thick and rich, or warmed for cold mornings. Or, for a special treat, form into cookie shape and dehydrate for a short while. It is delicious.

Onion Bread

This bread can be shaped by taking three long bread sticks and braiding them together.
It looks elegant and tastes divine.

2 cups soft white spring wheat (sprouted)
1/2 – 1 finely minced yellow onion
1/2 cup finely minced fresh parsley
1 – 2 tsp Onion Magic
1 – 2 tsp rosemary
2 – 3 tsp vege-sal or Spike

Machine Instructions

Put the closed blank screen over the twin gears. Then attach the pulp discharge casing without the outlet adjusting knob. Place a large enough bowl to catch the droppings from the outlets.

Instructions

1. Soak the wheat berries for 8 – 12 hours and rinse. Let sprout for 12 – 24 hours, until a small tail emerges, rinsing as necessary.
2. Put the wheat through the machine and into a bowl.
3. Stir the finely minced onions and parsley into the mixture, spicing to taste with Onion Magic, rosemary and vege-sal.
4. Form into three long braids, not more than 1 – 1-1/2-inches thick, and braid them together into a loaf, or two small loaves. Let dry in the sun 6 – 10 hours, or dehydrate at 105°F for 10 – 16 hours.
5. Serve warm or store in a plastic bag in the refrigerator. Lovely served with soup or salad. Garnish with vegetables.

Soaking time: 8 – 12 hours
Sprouting time: 12 – 24 hours
Preparation time: 20 minutes
Dehydrating time: 6 – 16 hours
Yields: 1 long or 2 short loaves

Preparation Hints

This tasty loaf can be garnished with some of the onions. This is a delicious variation because the onions become sweeter from the dehydration.

Barley Warmed Spaghetti

This does stretch the imagination to call it spaghetti, but it can be dehydrated and made into crunchy noodles and served with Presto Pesto.

2 cups barley (soak 4 -6 hours, rinse)
2 – 4 tsp olive oil
1/2 cup fresh basil
2 – 3 tsp vege-sal

Machine instructions
Put the machine together for making pasta. Instead of using the twin gears, secure the pasta screw and pasta guide in the twin gears housing. Attach the pasta screen, set at chosen noodle size, to the pasta guide. Then put on the pasta output attachment. Now you are ready to make pasta.

Preparation and Serving Instructions
1. Soak the barley 4 – 6 hours, rinse.
2. Stir all the ingredients together in a bowl, and slowly spoon the mixture into the machine catching the pasta on a dehydrator tray, pinching off at the desired length, or catching it all in a bowl.
3. Set the dehydrator at 105°F, and dehydrate noodles until crisp, about 2 – 4 hours, depending on weather and climate.
4. Serve fresh or warm, with Presto Pesto or That's a My Tomato Sauce.

Soaking time: 4 – 6 hours
Preparation time: 20 minutes
Dehydrating time: 2 – 4 hours
Yields: 2 – 4 servings

Preparation Hints
This dish can be eaten fresh out of the machine. I prefer mine slightly warmed in the dehydrator; take your pick.

Russian Rye Crackers

The omega 3 and 6 oils in the flax, plus the calcium and protein in the sunflower seeds makes them a crunchy delight.

2 cups rye

1 cup sunflower seeds

1/2 cup caraway seeds

1/2 cup flax seeds

1 – 2 tsp vege-sal

1 tsp Onion Magic

1/2 tsp granulated garlic (optional)

Machine Instructions

Put the closed blank screen over the twin gears. Then attach the pulp discharge casing without the outlet adjusting knob. Place a large enough bowl to catch the droppings from the outlet.

Preparation and Serving Instructions

1. In a large bowl, soak the rye, sunflower, caraway and flax seeds together for 8 – 12 hours, pouring off the excess water through a strainer with a fine mesh.
2. Slowly spoon this mixture through the machine and into a bowl.
3. Stir spices into the mixture to taste. Spread the mixture out onto dehydrator trays, covered with teflex, or wax paper. Spread 1/4-inch thick, in a rectangular shape, and cut it with a spatula into crackers 2 by 2-inches or as you prefer.
4. Set the dehydrator at 105°F and dehydrate until crisp, about 12 – 16 hours, depending on weather and climate. Check occasionally, rescore and turn over, taking off the teflex sheet (or wax paper) when the first half is done.
5. Serve warm or store in covered containers.

Soaking time: 8 – 12 hours
Preparation time: 20 minutes
Dehydrating time: 12 – 16 hours
Yields: 40 – 60 crackers (at least 2 trays full)

Preparation Hints

Flax seeds do not break up too much in the machine which is important because flax is delicate and dehydrates better whole. The mixture dehydrates well because flax becomes gelatinous.

Such a Sunny Rye Bread

I first made this sourdough-flavored bread in Santa Monica for a dinner workshop. I let one loaf dry in the sun and the other in the dehydrator. They both tasted lovely. The one in the sun was moist like essene breads.

4 cups rye
(soaked 8 – 12 hours, rinsed; sprouted 12 – 24 hours)

2 cups sunflower seeds
(soaked 8 – 12 hours, rinsed)

2 – 3 tsp ground caraway seeds

2 – 3 tsp ground dill seed

2 – 3 tsp vege-sal

fresh dill weed

Machine Instructions

Put the closed blank screen over the twin gears. Then attach the pulp discharge casing without the outlet adjusting knob. Place a large enough bowl to catch the droppings from the outlet.

Preparation and Serving Instructions

1. Soak rye for 8 – 12 hours, rinse, and let sprout for 12 – 24 hours. Soak the sunflower seeds separately for 8 – 12 hours and rinse.
2. Alternate putting the rye, sunflower seeds and caraway seeds through the machine and into a bowl.
3. Stir the mixture, spicing to taste with the ground dill seeds and vege-sal.
4. Form into two long narrow loaves, not more than 1 – 1-1/2-inches thick, garnishing with either vegetables or fresh dill. Let dry in the sun 6 – 10 hours or dehydrate on a tray at 105°F for 10 – 16 hours.
5. Serve warm or store in a plastic bag in the refrigerator. Best served with soup or salad.

Soaking time: 8 – 12 hours
Sprouting time: 12 – 24 hours
Preparation time: 20 minutes
Dehydrating time: 6 – 16 hours
Yields: 2 loaves

Preparation Hints

Dry the sunflower seeds for a bit before putting them through the machine or the dough can be sticky if the rye and sunflower seeds are both wet.

Rockin' Rye Bread Sticks

The crunch of a bread stick is a satisfying sensation. These have both an outer crunch and the inner softness. What a delight!

2 cups rye
(soaked 8 – 12 hours, rinsed; sprouted 12 – 24 hours)

1 cup sunflower seeds
(soaked 8 – 12 hours, rinsed)

1/2 cup caraway seeds

2 – 3 tsp Onion Magic

2 – 3 tsp vege-sal

Machine Instructions
Put the closed blank screen over the twin gears and then attach the pulp discharge casing with the rice cake guide securely in place. Put a tray to catch the bread sticks dough from the outlet.

Preparation and Serving Instructions
1. Soak the rye for 8 – 12 hours, rinse, and let sprout for 12 – 24 hours, until a small tail emerges, rinsing as necessary. Soak the sunflower seeds separately for 8 – 12 hours and rinse.
2. Stir all the ingredients together in a bowl, and slowly spoon the mixture into the machine catching the bread sticks on a dehydrator tray, pinching off at the desired length.
3. Let dry in the sun 6 – 10 hours, or dehydrate at 105°F for 4 – 8 hours.
4. Serve warm or store in a plastic bag in the refrigerator. Best served with soup, salad or dip.

Soaking time: 8 – 12 hours
Sprouting time: 12 – 24 hours
Preparation time: 20 minutes
Dehydrating time: 4 – 8 hours
Yields: many bread sticks

Preparation Hints
This process works well with two people, one person to feed the machine, the other to catch the bread sticks, pinch off at the desired length, and catch the next one. This recipe drys quickly, so check regularly. Another preparation format is to braid two bread sticks together. It makes a lovely way to serve them.

Chapter XI
Besserts and Other Sweet Treats

Chewy Carob Cookies

These are named after one of their best qualities, chewiness. Finding raw carob powder can be difficult in some areas, but it can be ordered from most natural food stores.

2 cups walnuts
1 cup organic raisins
2 – 3 Tbsp raw carob powder

Machine Instructions
Put the closed blank screen over the twin gears and then put the pulp discharge casing on without the outlet adjusting knob. Place a large enough bowl to catch the droppings from the outlet.

Preparation and Serving Instructions
1. Soak the raisins in warm water for 10 – 20 minutes. Save the soaking water.
2. In a bowl, stir together all the ingredients, with enough of the soaking water to make a paste with the carob powder.
3. Put the mixture through the machine and into a bowl.
4. With a spoon, drop the dough (about one tablespoon per cookie) on dehydrator trays with a teflex sheet, and dehydrate at 105°F for 12 – 24 hours, turning over when dough is firm.
5. Serve warm.

Soaking time: 10 – 20 minutes
Preparation time: 25 minutes
Dehydrating time: 12 – 24 hours
Yields: 20 – 35 cookies

Preparation Hints
The thickness of this cookie makes it crunchy and the drop method creates a macaroon shape.

Macadamian Sweetie

I first tasted macadamia nuts in Hawaii. What a memorable treat. These cookies are rich and delightful. The fresh apple makes these cookies soft, so they do not have to be dehydrated as long. In fact, the dough tastes so good, it can be eaten raw.

2 cups macadamia nuts

1/4 – 1/2 apple

1/2 – 1 cup raisins

Machine Instructions

Put the closed blank screen over the twin gears and then put the pulp discharge casing on without the outlet adjusting knob. Place a large enough bowl to catch the dough from the outlet.

Preparation and Serving Instructions

1. Alternate putting the macadamia nuts, apple and raisins through the machine into a bowl.
2. With a spoon, drop the dough (about one tablespoon per cookie) on dehydrator trays with a teflex sheet, and dehydrate at 105°F for 8 –12 hours, turning over when dough is firm.

3. Serve warm.

Preparation time: 25 minutes
Dehydrating time: 8 – 12 hours
Yields: 20 – 35 cookies

Preparation Hints

If you want a moister cookie, add more apple. Otherwise, add less apple and test the consistency of the dough. The raisins make this a sweet cookie, so add more or less to suit your taste.

Date Nut Torte

My friend, Beverly Peterson, showed me how to make a version of this rich dessert.
It can be made with soaked almonds, walnuts or macadamias.

Frosting

1 cup pitted dates
2 Tbsp lemon juice
1 tsp lemon rind
1/4 – 1/2 cup water

Filling

2 cups pecans
2 cups raisins
2 cups filberts (hazelnuts)
2 cups currants
1 lemon (for decorating)

Machine Instructions (For making the filling)
Put the closed blank screen over the twin gears and then put the pulp discharge casing on without the outlet adjusting knob. Place a large enough bowl to catch the dough from the outlet.

Preparation and Serving Instructions
1. For the lemon date frosting: in a blender mix until smooth the pitted dates, lemon juice, using enough water to thin, stirring the lemon rind into the frosting at the end.
2. For the bottom layer: alternate putting the pecans and raisins into the machine and into a bowl. Press into a round shape about 1-inch thick and 8-inches in diameter.
3. Frost the top side of the first layer of the torte with 1/2 the frosting, saving the rest for frosting the top.
4. For the top layer: alternate putting the filberts and currants into the machine and into a bowl. On a piece of wax paper, press the mixture into a round shape to fit on top of the bottom layer, and carefully place on top of the frosted layer.
5. Frost the entire outside, decorating with lemon slices around the edge.
6. Serve or chill and serve.

Preparation time: 20 minutes
Yields: 8 – 12 servings

Preparation Hints
The nuts and fruit get moist after being blended by the Green Power machine. Pecans release a fair amount of oil after being processed. If desired, press it out with a paper towel. It could be easily formed into a heart shape as well, making a perfect Valentine's Day torte.

Oatmeal Cookie

These are a thicker, sweeter version of the traditional oatmeal cookie.

2 cups oat groats
(soaked 4 – 6 hours, rinsed)
1 cup pitted dates
1/2 cup organic raisins

Frosting
1 banana
4 – 6 pitted dates
1/4 – 1/2 cup water

Machine Instructions
Put the closed blank screen over the twin gears and then put the pulp discharge casing on without the outlet adjusting knob. Place a large enough bowl to catch the dough from the outlet.

Preparation and Serving Instructions
1. Soak the oat groats 4 – 6 hours, rinse.
2. Alternate putting the oats, pitted dates and raisins through the machine and into a bowl.
3. Take the dough and roll it out between two pieces of wax paper, and cut out into cookie shapes, or hand form into cookies 1/4 – 1/2-inch thick.
4. In a blender, mix the banana and pitted dates with enough water to blend, keeping the frosting mixture thick. Brush on top of cookies.
5. Put cookies on dehydrator trays, and dehydrate at 105°F for 6 – 10 hours, or until desired crispness, turning over when the dough is firm.
6. Serve warm, with extra sauce available for dipping.

Soaking time: 4 – 6 hours
Preparation time: 25 minutes
Dehydrating time: 6 – 10 hours
Yields: 20 – 35 cookies

Preparation Hints
To make the cookies dark on one side, add raw carob powder to the frosting and frost the other side after turning. What a festive cookie platter!

Grainy Cookies

Here is an alternative cookie recipe for those folks with a sensitivity to wheat. Kamut is a large grain that is quite tasty, and can be found in most natural food stores.

1 cup kamut

(soaked 8 – 12 hours, rinsed, sprouted 12 – 24 hours)

1/4 cup pitted dates

1/2 cup currants

Spice options: cinnamon and/or nutmeg

Machine Instructions

Put the closed blank screen over the twin gears and then put the pulp discharge casing on without the outlet adjusting knob. Place a large enough bowl to catch the dough from the outlet.

Preparation and Serving Instructions

1. Soak the kamut for 8 – 12 hours, and rinse. Let sprout for 12 – 24 hours, rinsing as necessary.
2. Alternate putting the kamut, pitted dates and currants through the machine and into a bowl.
3. Stir dough, spicing with cinnamon and/or nutmeg to taste, and form into 1/4 – 1/2-inch thick cookies. Place on a dehydrator tray, dehydrating at 105°F for 6 – 10 hours, turning over when the top side is crisp and warm.
4. Serve warm.

Soaking time: 8 – 12 hours
Sprouting time: 12 – 24 hours
Preparation time: 20 minutes
Dehydrating time: 6 – 10 hours
Yields: 20 – 35 cookies

Preparation Hints

Pick soft rather than hard dates for this recipe. Medjool dates are wonderful.

Date with a Pecan

There are so many wonderful dishes to prepare with this lovely nut. Enjoy.

2 cups fresh pecans

6 – 10 pitted dates

Machine Instructions

Put the closed blank screen over the twin gears and then put the pulp discharge casing on without the outlet adjusting knob. Place a large enough bowl to catch the dough from the outlet.

Preparation and Serving Instructions

1. Alternate putting the dates and pecans through the machine and into a bowl.
2. Form into cookies and place on a dehydrator tray, dehydrating at 105°F for 6 – 10 hours, turning over when the top side is crisp and warm.
3. Serve warm.

Preparation time: 20 minutes
Dehydrating time: 6 – 10 hours
Yields: 20 – 35 cookies

Preparation Hints

This is a thicker, oily cookie dough, and can easily be molded by hand. Be playful and let yourself invent new shapes.

Picky Pecan Pie

This is a holiday favorite. Pecan pie sweet and filling, so a little goes a long way.

Crust
2 cups black mission figs
4 – 6 pitted dates

Filling
1 banana
1 cup pitted dates
2 cups pecans
1/4 cup shredded dehydrated unsweetened coconut

Machine Instructions
(For making the crust)
Put the closed blank screen over the twin gears and then put the pulp discharge casing on without the outlet adjusting knob. Place a large enough bowl to catch the dough from the outlet.

Preparation and Serving Instructions
1. Alternate putting the black mission figs and dates through the machine and into a bowl.
2. Press dough into a 9-inch pie plate and put into the refrigerator
3. For the filling: in a blender mix the banana, pitted dates, and 1 cup of pecans to desired thickness and pour half of the mixture on top of the crust, layer 1 cup of the chopped pecans on top, and spread the rest of the filling on top.
4. Decorate the top of the pie with shredded coconut and pecans.
5. Serve immediately or chill and serve.

Preparation time: 20 minutes
Yields: one 9-inch pie

Preparation Hints
You can make a softer crust by soaking the figs for an hour or so, then putting them through the machine (without the soaking water). Otherwise, the crust is a dark rich color and quite sweet. Sometimes, for cool winter nights, I will warm this pie up in the dehydrator for a short time.

Lemon Drop Cookies

This cookie brings out the best of the lemon flavor. Zest is the rind of the fruit. By using the fine part of any grater, the zest can be used.

2 cups almonds (soaked 8 – 12 hours)
1 lemon (organic)
6 – 10 pitted dates

Machine Instructions (For making the dough)
Put the closed blank screen over the twin gears and then put the pulp discharge casing on without the outlet adjusting knob. Place a large enough bowl to catch the dough from the outlet.

Preparation and Serving Instructions
1. Soak the almonds for 8 – 12 hours, and rinse.
2. Alternate putting the almonds and pitted dates through the machine and into a bowl.
3. Stir dough, spicing with 1 – 2 teaspoons of lemon zest and lemon juice. Drop the dough on a dehydrator tray, dehydrating at 105°F for 6 – 10 hours, turning over when the dough is firm.
4. Serve warm.

Soaking time: 8 – 12 hours
Preparation time: 20 minutes
Dehydrating time: 6 – 10 hours
Yields: 20 – 35 cookies

Preparation Hints
Using soft dates is best for this recipe. Getting the zest off the grater is best done with a soft brush. Brush the zest into a bowl and then spoon out only what you need.

Turkish Almond Delight

If you have never tasted a Turkish apricot before, this recipe is the best time to start. They are moister and sweeter. You can use ordinary apricots, but see if your natural food store can get these for you. It is worth the wait.

2 cups almonds (soaked 8 – 12 hours, rinsed)
1/2 – 1 cup Turkish apricots

Machine Instructions (For making the crust)
Put the closed blank screen over the twin gears and then put the pulp discharge casing on without the outlet adjusting knob. Place a large enough bowl to catch the dough from the outlet.

Preparation and Serving Instructions
1. Soak the almonds 8 – 12 hours, rinse.
2. Alternate putting the almonds and apricots through the machine and into a bowl.
3. Form into cookie shapes and eat fresh, or dehydrate on trays at 105°F for 6 – 12 hours, or until desired crispness.
4. Serve fresh or warmed.

Soaking time: 8 – 12 hours
Preparation time: 25 minutes
Yields: 20 – 35 cookies

Preparation Hints
These can be rolled out and pressed into cookie shapes as well.

137

Snow Ball Cookies

The beauty of these cookies is that they can be made during any season. The dried fruit makes this a non-seasonal free cookie. There are as many versions of this cookie as your imagination can create.

2 cups almonds
(8 – 12 hours soaked, rinsed)
1-1/2 cups your choice dried fruit
1 – 2 cups shredded unsweetened coconut

Machine Instructions

Put the closed blank screen over the twin gears and then put the pulp discharge casing on without the outlet adjusting knob. Place a large enough bowl to catch the dough from the outlet.

Preparation and Serving Instructions

1. Soak the almonds 8 – 12 hours, rinse.
2. Alternate putting the almonds and dried fruit through the machine and into a bowl, rolling the dough into balls.
3. In another bowl, put the dried coconut and coat the cookie dough into snow balls.
4. Serve on a festive platter.

Soaking time: 8 – 12 hours
Preparation time: 25 minutes
Yields: 20 – 35 cookies

Preparation Hints

These cookies are such fun to make. Be sure to cut the dried fruit into little pieces and use sparingly. If the machine gets stuck, just put the machine into reverse, by taking the on switch and pressing it down. You will hear the machine go on again, but this time the gears are going in the opposite direction. Then, turn it off and then on again. The machine will correct itself. If you limit which dried fruit you use, for example, first make a batch with only almonds and mango and then a batch with raisins and almonds, you can make a variety of flavors to enjoy. You might add more almonds to make a fairly large batch of cookies. These go quickly at any celebration so make lots.

Coconut Crunch Macaroons

A delicious cookie with a pleasing consistency. Look for non-alcoholic extracts to be found on the market.

2 cups almonds (soak 8 – 12 hours, rinse)

6 – 10 pitted dates

(soaked 2 hours, save the soaking water)

1 cup shredded dehydrated coconut

1 tsp almond extract (non-alcoholic)

Machine Instructions

Put the closed blank screen over the twin gears and then put the pulp discharge casing on without the outlet adjusting knob. Place a large enough bowl to catch the dough from the outlet.

Preparation and Serving Instructions

1. Soak the almonds 8 – 12 hours and rinse. Pit the dates and soak for 2 hours or so. Save the soaking water.
2. In a bowl, stir together all the ingredients, with 1/4 – 1/2 cup of the soaking water.
3. Put the mixture through the machine and into a bowl.
4. With a spoon, drop the dough (about one tablespoon per cookie) on dehydrator trays with a teflex sheet, and dehydrate at 105°F for 12 – 24 hours, turning over when dough is firm.
5. Serve warm.

Soaking time: 4 – 6 hours
Dehydrating time: 12 – 24 hours
Preparation time: 25 minutes
Yields: 20 – 35 cookies

Preparation Hints

The drop method of spooning out the dough makes for a thicker, chewier cookie. Watch that you do not make them too thick.

Barley Figgy Cookie

Remember fig newtons? This is the newer improved model—give it a try.

2 cups barley (soaked 4 – 6 hours, rinsed)

8 black mission figs

1/3 cup organic black raisins

(soaked until soft)

Frosting

1 banana

6 pitted dates

2 Tbsp raw carob powder

1/4 – 1/2 cup water

Machine Instruction

Put the closed blank screen over the twin gears and then attach the pulp discharge casing without the outlet adjusting knob. Place a large enough bowl to catch the droppings from the outlet.

Preparation and Serving Instructions

1. Soak the barley 4 – 6 hours, rinse.
2. Alternate putting the barley, figs and raisins through the machine and into a bowl.
3. Take the dough and roll it out between two pieces of wax paper. Cut out into cookie shapes or hand form into cookies 1/4 - 1/2-inch thick.
4. In a blender, mix the banana, pitted dates, carob powder and enough water to blend, keeping the frosting mixture thick. Brush on top of cookies.
5. Put cookies on dehydrator trays, and dehydrate at 105°F for 6 – 10 hours, or until desired crispness.
6. Serve warm, with sauce available for dipping.

Soaking time: 4 – 6 hours
Dehydrating time: 6 – 10 hours
Preparation time: 25 minutes
Yields: 20 – 35 cookies

Preparation Hints

Roll out the cookie dough between two sheets of wax paper to make this an easier task. Then peel off one layer of wax paper, cut the cookies and, using a spatula, place on the dehydrator trays.

Ambrosia Pie

The wonderful thing about this pie, other than its taste, is that it can be made and eaten in less than 30 minutes.

Crust
2 cups walnuts
4 – 6 pitted dates

Filling
2 cups of seedless organic grapes
2 apples
2 nectarines
1 banana
1/2 cup shredded dehydrated coconut

Machine Instructions
(for making the crust)
Put the closed blank screen over the twin gears and then put the pulp discharge casing on without the outlet adjusting knob. Place a large enough bowl to catch the dough from the outlet. You are ready to prepare the pie crust.

Preparation and Serving Instructions
1. Alternate putting the walnuts and dates through the machine and into a bowl.
2. Press dough into a 9-inch pie plate and put into the refrigerator
3. For the filling, in a blender mix the grapes, apples, nectarines, banana and 1/4 cup of coconut to desired thickness and pour on top of crust. Save some of the fruit for decorating the top.
4. Decorate the top of the pie with shredded coconut, sliced apples, grapes and nectarines.

Preparation time: 20 minutes
Yields: one 9-inch pie

Preparation Hints
For a thicker filling, add more banana.

141

Strawberry Cream Pie

I love strawberry pie, and this one is so much fun to prepare and decorate. We were visiting a friend in Silver City and I made two of these pies. Both were gone before the end of the evening. Even, the next door neighbor got in on the action.

Crust

2 cups almonds
(soak 8 – 12 hours, rinse)

4 – 6 pitted dates

Filling

5 bananas

1 box strawberries

2 kiwis

1/2 – 1 cup currants

1 lemon

Machine Instructions
(For making the dough)
Put the closed blank screen over the twin gears and then put the pulp discharge casing on without the outlet adjusting knob. Place a large enough bowl to catch the dough from the outlet.

Preparation and Serving Instructions
1. Soak almonds 8 – 12 hours, rinse.
2. Alternate putting the almonds and dates through the machine and into a bowl.
2. Press dough into a 9-inch pie plate, then cover the bottom of the crust with two sliced bananas and put into the refrigerator
3. For the filling, in a blender mix two of the bananas, 3/4 box of strawberries, 1 kiwi, 1/2 cup of currants to desired thickness, spicing with lemon juice to taste, and pour on top of crust (save some of the fruit for decorating the top).
4. Decorate the top of the pie with banana, strawberries, kiwi, currants and lemon slices.
5. Serve fresh, or chill and serve.

Preparation time: 25 minutes
Yields: one 9-inch pie

Preparation Hints
When you pick out strawberries, they should smell sweet. Most fruits have a wonderful aroma when they are ripe.

Rawcous Apple Pie

Could anything be more basic than apple pie? This one is so good, I know you will enjoy making it for parties, holidays and whenever the mood strikes you.

Crust
2 cups walnuts
4 – 6 pitted dates

Filling
4 – 5 apples
2 bananas
1 cup currants
1 lemon
cinnamon

Machine Instructions
(For making the crust)
Put the closed blank screen over the twin gears and then put the pulp discharge casing on without the outlet adjusting knob. Place a large enough bowl to catch the dough from the outlet.

Preparation and Serving Instructions
1. Alternate putting the walnuts and dates through the machine and into a bowl.
2. Press dough into a 9-inch pie plate, line the bottom with one finely sliced apple sprinkled with lemon juice, and put into the refrigerator
3. For the filling: in a blender mix 2 apples, 1 banana and most of the currants to desired thickness, spicing with lemon juice and cinnamon, and pour on top of crust (save some of the fruit for decorating the top).
4. Decorate the top of the pie with finely sliced apple, banana, currants and lemon slices.
5. Serve fresh or warmed.

Preparation time: 20 minutes
Yields: one 9-inch pie

Preparation Hints
To make the filling thicker add more banana, less fresh apples. Lemon juice prevents the apples from turning brown. Try Fuji or Delicious apples when they are in season.

Lemon Cream Pie

Lemons are wonderful for stimulating our livers to make enzymes. This pie is delicately flavored by both the juice and the zest. A true mid-summer's dream cream pie.

2 cup black mission figs
4 frozen bananas
3 fresh bananas
2 lemons

Machine Instructions
(For making the sorbet filling)
Put the closed blank screen over the twin gears and then put the pulp discharge casing on without the outlet adjusting knob. Place a large enough bowl to catch the sorbet from the outlet.

Preparation and Serving Instructions
1. Freeze the fruit the night before (or at least for 12 hours).
2. For the crust, put the black mission figs through the machine, then press into a 9-inch pie plate and freeze for 1 – 2 hours.
3 For the filling, alternate putting the fresh and frozen bananas through the machine and into a bowl. Stir in the lemon zest and fresh lemon juice to taste. Pour mixture into the frozen pie crust.
4. Put in the freezer for 2 – 4 hours.
5. When ready to serve, decorate with sliced fresh bananas and lemons. Let soften in the refrigerator 30 minutes or so and serve.

Freezing time: 12 hours, 3 – 5 hours after prepared
Preparation time: 20 minutes
Yields: one 9-inch pie

Preparation Hints
Play with the timing so that this sorbet pie is served frozen but soft. If you like harder sorbet, freeze it longer.

Lemon Zest Pudding

I first made this for a Jewish holiday.
We served it warm in a pie plate.
People thought it was cooked, but it
was not, just dehydrated overnight.
The secret to its success was
serving it warm.

1 cup almonds (soaked 8 – 12 hours, rinsed)

1 cup pitted prunes

1 cup organic raisins

2 lemons

Sauce

2 cups currants

Machine Instructions (For making the pudding)
Put the closed blank screen over the twin gears
and then put the pulp discharge casing on
without the outlet adjusting knob. Place a large
enough bowl to catch the pudding from the
outlet.

Preparation and Serving Instructions
1. Soak the almonds 8 – 12 hours, rinse.
2. Alternate putting the almonds, prunes and
   raisins through the machine and into a bowl.
3. Stir the mixture, spicing with lemon juice and
   1 – 2 teaspoons of lemon rind (zest) to taste.
   Pour into a glass pie plate and put in the
   dehydrator at 105°F for 6 – 10 hours.
4. For the sauce: in a blender mix the currants
   with enough water to blend into a thick
   smooth consistency. Warm in a separate dish in
   the dehydrator.
5. Serve warm with the currant sauce on top.

Preparation time: 20 minutes
Dehydration time: 6 – 10 hours
Yields: one 9-inch pie

Preparation Hints
This pie can be eaten as is, but on a cold day,
warm is wonderful.

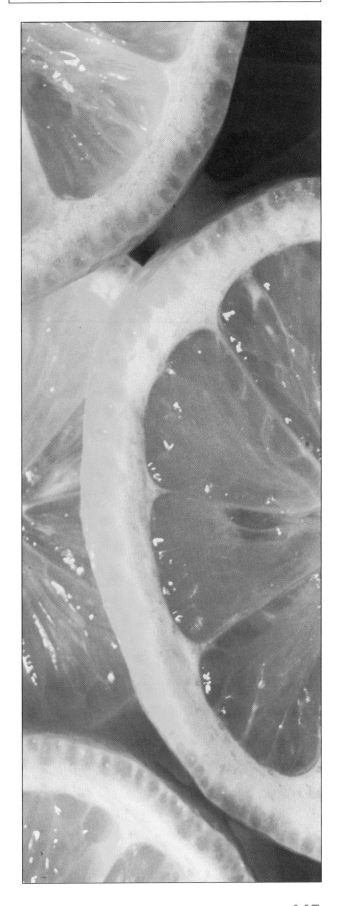

Passionate Persimmon Pudding

I look forward to the fall when persimmons are in season. This pudding is best made with the soft persimmons. Make sure they are soft or you will be puckering for quite a while. The ginger is warming for the blood. A great breakfast pudding.

3 – 4 fresh soft persimmons
2 pears
1 – 2 slices fresh ginger
1/2 cup soaked currants
(soak in warm water 10 – 20 minutes)

Machine Instructions
(For making the pudding)
Put the closed blank screen over the twin gears and then put the pulp discharge casing on without the outlet adjusting knob. Place a large enough bowl to catch the pudding from the outlet.

Preparation and Serving Instructions
1. Soak the currants in warm water for 10 – 20 minutes.
2. Alternate putting the persimmon, pear and ginger through the machine and into a bowl, and stir the mixture.

3. Serve garnished with the soaked currants on top.

Soaking time: 10 – 20 minutes
Preparation time: 10 minutes
Yields: 4 servings

Preparation Hints
The smoothness of this pudding is from the ripeness of the persimmon. Be sure to start with less ginger as it can have an overpowering taste.

Key Lime Parfait

There is something cheerful about the colors of this dessert. This dessert is best served before the meal, not afterwards. The fruits digest so quickly and it sets a lovely tone for the meal.

3 frozen persimmons
4 frozen bananas
1 fresh banana
1 lime

Machine Instructions
(For making the sorbet)
Put the closed blank screen over the twin gears and then put the pulp discharge casing on with the rice cake outlet adjusting knob. Place a bowl to catch the round tubes of sorbet from the outlet.

Preparation and Serving Instructions
1. Freeze the fruit the night before (or at least for 12 hours). Persimmons can be frozen without peeling their skins, just cut off the tops before freezing.
2. For the first layer, alternate putting 2 frozen bananas, 1 fresh banana and 1 – 2 teaspoons of lime zest through the machine and into a bowl. Put into parfait glasses and put into the freezer.
3. For the second layer: alternate putting 2 frozen bananas and the frozen persimmons through the machine and into a bowl. Put on top of the first layer and freeze for 1 – 2 hours, or serve immediately.

Freezing time: 12 hours, 1 – 2 hours after prepared
Preparation time: 20 minutes
Yields: 4 – 6 servings

Preparation Hints
The beauty of this recipe is that frozen persimmons do not have to be ripe. Something about freezing them hastens their ripening.

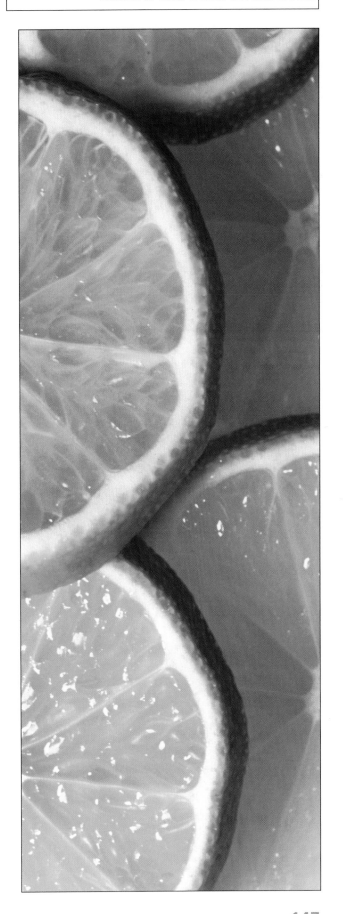

Kiberry Cream Pie or Parfait

Kiwi and strawberries are lovely together. This double decker sorbet pie is both refreshing and impressive to serve at any gathering. Or, you could make individual servings and call it parfait.

6 fresh bananas

4 frozen bananas

1 box frozen strawberries

1 cup fresh strawberries

2 frozen kiwis

1 fresh kiwi

4 pitted dates

Machine Instructions
(For making the sorbet filling)
Put the closed blank screen over the twin gears and then put the pulp discharge casing on without the outlet adjusting knob. Place a large enough bowl to catch the sorbet from the outlet.

Preparation and Serving Instructions
1. Freeze the fruit the night before (or at least for 12 hours). Take the skin off the bananas and kiwis, and the tops off the strawberries.
2. For the crust, slice and mash fresh bananas and spread evenly into a 9-inch pie plate. Put into the freezer.
3. For the first layer, alternate putting 2 frozen bananas, 1 fresh banana, and frozen strawberries through the machine and into a bowl. Put on top of the banana crust and put into the freezer.
4. For the second layer, alternate putting 2 frozen bananas and the frozen kiwis through the machine into a bowl. Put on top of the first layer and freeze for 3 – 6 hours.

5. Decorate the top with fresh sliced bananas, strawberries and kiwis and let soften in the refrigerator for an hour or so, and serve.

Freezing time: 12 hours, 3 – 6 hours after prepared, 1 hour refrigerator time
Preparation time: 20 minutes
Yields: 4 – 6 servings

Preparation Hints
The key to success is getting each layer firm enough before putting the next layer on top. The crust is fine, even if it is soft when the first layer goes on top, but the strawberry layer (the first) needs to be firm before putting the kiwi layer on top. This can be decorated so beautifully, making mandala or concentric rings type patterns. If you are making the parfait version of this, put the mashed bananas in the bottom of the glass, then layer in the colors as you would the pie. Set for 20 minutes or so, and serve at desired consistency. The beauty of this version is that you do not have to cut this to serve your guests. It can be made ahead of time and looks delightful.

Blueberry Sorbet

Fresh and frozen blueberries can be used for this sorbet. The trick is to keep the gears cold and not make the mixture too thin or warm. For summer, this is one of the treats I enjoy serving to friends who like ice cream - a healthier choice.

4 frozen bananas
1 box frozen blueberries
1/2 – 1 cup fresh blueberries

Machine Instructions
(For making the sorbet)
Put the closed blank screen over the twin gears and then put the pulp discharge casing on with the rice cake outlet adjusting knob. Place a bowl to catch the round tubes of sorbet from the outlet.

Instructions
1. Freeze the fruit the night before (or at least for 12 hours).
2. Alternate putting the frozen blueberries and bananas through the machine, occasionally putting a few fresh ones through into a bowl. Be sure to keep the gears cold or this will turn into a slush.
3. Serve immediately, or put in the freezer for 10 – 20 minutes and serve.

Freezing time: 12 hours
Preparation time: 20 minutes
Yields: 4 – 6 servings

Preparation Hints
Keeping the fruit frozen is the key to making this dish. Use a dash of lemon zest on top as a taste treat. Catching the sorbet as it comes out the rice cake attachment can be half the fun of making this dish.

Winter Sorbet

Spiced with cinnamon and nutmeg, this is fitting at any holiday gathering. Serve this bessert before the meal because it is all fruit. It sets a sweet tone for the evening.

4 frozen persimmons
3 frozen bananas
1 fresh banana
cinnamon
nutmeg

Machine Instructions
(For making the sorbet)
Put the closed blank screen over the twin gears and then put the pulp discharge casing on with the rice cake outlet adjusting knob. Place a bowl to catch the round tubes of sorbet from the outlet.

Preparation and Serving Instructions
1. Freeze the fruit the night before (or at least for 12 hours). Persimmons can be frozen in their skins, just cut off the tops before freezing.
2. Alternate putting the frozen persimmons, 2 frozen bananas and 1 fresh banana through the machine and into a bowl. Add a dash of cinnamon and nutmeg into the machine.
3. Serve immediately.

Freezing time: 12 hours
Preparation time: 20 minutes
Yields: 6 – 8 servings

Preparation Hints
The fresh banana makes this a softer dessert. You can keep this more frozen by either leaving out the fresh banana, or by putting it back into the freezer for 30 minutes or so. This allows you to make it ahead of time and serve the guests as they arrive.

Blushing Sorbet

Finding sweet strawberries is important. They are ripe if they smell sweet in the box.

2 frozen bananas
1 box frozen strawberries
1 cup fresh strawberries
spearmint leaves

Machine Instructions
(For making the sorbet)
Put the closed blank screen over the twin gears and then put the pulp discharge casing on with the rice cake outlet adjusting knob. Place a bowl to catch the round tubes of sorbet from the outlet.

Preparation and Serving Instructions
1. Freeze the fruit the night before (or at least for 12 hours).
2. Alternate putting the frozen strawberries and bananas through the machine and into a bowl.

3. Serve immediately, garnishing with fresh strawberries and spearmint leaves, or put in the freezer for 10 – 20 minutes and serve.

Freezing time: 12 hours
Preparation time: 20 minutes
Yields: 4 – 6 servings

Preparation Hints
This can be made ahead, served in parfait glasses or pudding dishes. If it gets too hard in the freezer, put the dishes in the refrigerator and let the sorbet soften.

Summer Sorbet

What could make a more tasty sorbet than the summer fruits of mangoes and pineapple. I added bananas to my recipe. Try making it either way and see which you enjoy.

2 frozen mangoes

1/2 frozen pineapple

2 frozen bananas

1 lemon

Machine Instructions (For making the sorbet) Put the closed blank screen over the twin gears and then put the pulp discharge casing on with the rice cake outlet adjusting knob. Place a bowl to catch the round tubes of sorbet from the outlet.

Preparation and Serving Instructions
1. Freeze the fruit the night before (or at least for 12 hours). Cut and prepare the mangoes and pineapples before freezing.
2. Alternate putting 2 frozen bananas, mangoes, pineapple and 1 – 2 teaspoons lemon zest through the machine and into a bowl.
3. Serve immediately, garnished with fresh lemon slices.

Freezing time: 12 hours
Preparation time: 20 minutes
Yields: 6 – 8 servings

Preparation Hints
The lemon zest is magical in this recipe. You can stir it into the finished product or let it go through the machine.

Orange You in the Pink Sorbet

A fall sorbet, or freeze the persimmons in season and surprise your friends during the summer with a persimmon-strawberry double layered orange and pink dessert.

4 frozen persimmons

4 frozen bananas

3 fresh bananas

2 cups frozen strawberries

fresh mint leaves

Machine Instructions (For making the sorbet) Put the closed blank screen over the twin gears and then put the pulp discharge casing on with the rice cake outlet adjusting knob. Place a bowl to catch the round tubes of sorbet from the outlet.

Preparation and Serving Instructions
1. Freeze the fruit the night before (or at least for 12 hours). Persimmons can be frozen and blended without peeling their skins.
2. For the first layer, alternate putting 2 frozen bananas, 1 fresh banana, and persimmons through the machine and into a bowl. Put into parfait glasses and put into the freezer for 30 minutes.
3. For the second layer, alternate putting 2 frozen bananas and the frozen strawberries through the machine and into a bowl. Put on top of the first layer. Serve immediately or freeze for 1 – 2 hours.

Freezing time: 12 hours, 1 – 2 hours after prepared
Preparation time: 20 minutes
Yields: 4 – 6 servings

Preparation Hints
Getting the sorbet in narrow glasses can be a challenge. One suggestion is to use a pastry tube and squeeze it into the glass. Otherwise, just spoon it into whatever lovely serving dish suits you and enjoy the sunrise of colors created by this dessert.

Berry Yummy Pudding

Berry season offers many lovely fruits from which to choose from. Pick your favorite berry and make this pudding a favorite.

3 bananas

1 box fresh berries

(strawberries, blueberries, blackberries

or raspberries)

fresh spearmint leaves

Machine Instructions (For making the pudding) Put the open blank screen over the twin gears and then put the pulp discharge casing on without the outlet adjusting knob. Place a large enough bowl to catch the pudding from both openings.

Preparation and Serving Instructions
1. Alternate putting the fruits through the machine and into a bowl.
2. Stir with a whisk.
3. Serve in a bowl, garnished with fresh spearmint leaves.

Preparation time: 10 minutes
Yields: 4 servings

Preparation Hints
This can be made with more than one type of berry. You can make a lovely pudding if you separate the colors, and pour them in rings in the bowl. A berry pretty pudding indeed!

Carob Mint Pie

This is a must for parties, especially if you like mint. It looks like a chocolate cream pie, but the carob will not interfere with calcium absorption, and the carob flavor is heavenly with the banana.

Crust

2 cups soaked almonds
(soaked 8 – 12 hours, rinsed)

4 – 6 pitted dates

Filling

4 frozen bananas

3 fresh bananas

3 Tbsp carob powder
(raw if you can find it, otherwise roasted)

1 – 2 tsp mint extract
(non-alcoholic variety)

spearmint leaves

carob chips

Machine Instructions
(For making the crust)
Put the closed blank screen over the twin gears and then put the pulp discharge casing on without the outlet adjusting knob. Place a large enough bowl to catch the dough from the outlet.

Machine Instructions
(For making the sorbet filling)
Put the closed blank screen over the twin gears and then put the pulp discharge casing on without the outlet adjusting knob. Place a large enough bowl to catch the sorbet from the outlet.

Preparation and Serving Instructions
1. Freeze the fruit the night before (or at least for 12 hours).
2. Soak almonds 8 – 12 hours, rinse.
3. For the crust, alternate putting the almonds and dates through the machine, then press into a 9-inch pie plate and freeze for 1 – 2 hours.

4. For the filling, mash up the fresh banana stirring in the carob powder and the mint extract. Then, alternate putting the fresh and frozen bananas through the machine and into a bowl, and pour this into the frozen pie crust.
5. Put in the freezer for 2 – 4 hours.
6. When ready to serve, decorate with sliced fresh bananas, carob chips and mint leaves. Let soften in the refrigerator 30 minutes and serve.

Freezing time: 12 hours, 3 – 5 hours after prepared
Preparation time: 20 minutes
Yields: one 9-inch pie

Preparation Hints
Timing is the challenge of this recipe, but once done, it gets simpler. Use a fork to stir in the carob powder with the fresh banana. The more carob powder you use, the darker the pie will be. Use whatever amount you prefer to get the desired color.

Tropical Pie

There is something so exotic about mangoes that tasting this pie made with fresh pineapple and mangoes whisks me away to a desert island. Where does it take you?

Crust

2 – 2-1/2 cups calimari figs

(the light colored ones)

Filling

2 peeled, sliced mangoes

1/2 peeled sliced pineapple

4 bananas

1/2 cup fresh blackberries

or raspberries

Topping

mango, kiwi, banana, blueberries, raspberries

Machine Instructions for making the crust
Put the closed blank screen over the twin gears and then put the pulp discharge casing on without the outlet adjusting knob. Place a large enough bowl to catch the dough from the outlet.

Preparation and Serving Instructions
1. Alternate putting the figs through the machine and into a bowl.
2. Press dough into a 9-inch pie plate, slice two bananas and cover the crust. Put into the refrigerator.
3. For the filling: in a blender mix 3/4 of the mango, pineapple and two bananas to desired thickness and pour on top of crust (save some of the fruit for decorating the top).

4. Decorate the top of the pie with mangoes, pineapple, kiwi, banana, blueberries and raspberries.
5. Serve fresh, or chill and serve.

Preparation time: 20 minutes
Yields: one 9-inch pie

Preparation Hints
A decorating tip: take the mango, kiwi, pineapple, berries and banana and cut out shapes with small cookie cutters.

Yam I Am Pie

This is Dr. Gabriel's favorite holiday pie. I traveled to Arizona a few years ago to make this pie for their Thanksgiving celebration. Everyone there loved it. Maybe you will too.

Crust
2 cups pecans
4 – 6 pitted dates

Filling
2 peeled yams
1 cup pine nuts
4 – 5 pitted soft dates
cinnamon
nutmeg

Machine Instructions
(For making the crust and the filling)
Put the closed blank screen over the twin gears and then put the pulp discharge casing on without the outlet adjusting knob. Place a large enough bowl to catch the dough and/or filling from the outlet.

Preparation and Serving Instructions
1. Alternate putting the pecans and dates through the machine and into a bowl.
2. Press dough into a 9-inch pie plate and put into the dehydrator.
3. For the filling: in the machine alternate putting the yams, pine nuts and dates through, stir mixture, spice to taste with the cinnamon and nutmeg, and pour on top of crust.
4. Decorate the top of the pie with pecans.
5. Warm the pie in the dehydrator at 105°F for 2 – 6 hours, or to desired temperature.

Preparation time: 20 minutes
Dehydration time: 2 – 6 hours
Yields: one 9-inch pie

Preparation Hints
Do not leave in the dehydrator too long, as the pie could sour. The pecans can make the crust oily so press it out with a paper towel and then form the crust. Or, try a crust of almonds and dates.

Fruit Crêpes and Roll-Ups

160		
Black Lovlies calimari and black mission figs		**Iron Maiden** banana, apricots, raisins
Cranberried Crêpes banana, dried cranberries, applesauce		**Raisin Rolls** banana, golden raisins, black raisins
Guava Growl Roll banana, dried guava		**Rhody's Banana Crêpe** banana, papaya
Freshly Dated banana, dates, dried mango		**Tropical Princess** banana, mango, pineapple

These desserts are only the natural fruit. I enjoy making these for a sweet snack when I am about to go on the road. It seems odd to take a dry fruit, add water, and reform it again, but the mixture of some of these flavors is worth the time invested. These recipes are simple to make. Simply soak the dried fruit, blend in the machine, pour onto a teflex or wax sheet and dehydrate until dry enough to roll up and enjoy as a fruit roll. The more frozen fruit you add, the thicker the fruit roll. Fresh bananas make it thinner, creamier and sweeter.

The fruit crêpe has many possibilities. You can put any kind of fresh fruit, sauce or filling you desire into these soft sweet desserts. You could use any of the fruit rolls, dehydrating them less to keep them thin and soft. There is something so delectable about its texture combined with crisp fresh fruit, smothered in a pudding-like sauce. On top of the recipes suggested, make up your own with your favorite fruits. These store well in ziplock plastic bags, and are a real treat for those who love sweets.

For every recipe, the machine and preparation instructions are the same.

Machine Instructions
Put the closed blank screen over the twin gears and then put the pulp discharge casing on without the outlet adjusting knob. Place a bowl to catch the fruit from the outlet.

Preparation Instructions
1. Soak the dried fruit in warm water until soft, 20 minutes—2 hours at most.
2. Put the fruit through the machine and into a bowl.
3. Spread the mixture evenly on a dehydrator tray, on top of a teflex sheet, or waxed paper and dehydrate at 105°F to the desired consistency (12 – 24 hours). Turn over when firm, and remove the teflex or wax paper to allow the other side to dehydrate.
4. Roll up and serve warm or store in containers. Store in a cool dry place.
5. Each batch yields one sheet of fruit roll.

Black and Beige Lovlies

2 cups black mission figs

2 cups calimari figs

(the light colored ones)

Make one sheet of each fruit and roll up together.

Cranberried Crêpes

Crêpe

2 cups dried cranberries

1 banana

Stuffing

apple slices and apple sauce, cinnamon

Guava Growl Roll

2 bananas

1 cup dried guava

(can be soaked or not)

Freshly Dated

2 fresh bananas

6 pitted dates (do not soak)

1 cup dried mangoes

Iron Maiden

2 bananas

1/2 cup dried apricots

(Turkish are the best)

1/2 cup golden raisins

Raisin Rolls

4 fresh bananas

1 cup golden raisins

1 cup black raisins

Use two bananas and one cup of raisins for each sheet, create one of each color and roll together.

Rhody's Banana Crêpe

Crêpe

3 bananas

Stuffing

papaya, banana

Tropical Princess

2 frozen bananas

1/2 cup dried mango

1/2 cup dried pineapple

For the Green Life and Green Power machines:

Green Power International
14109 Pontlavoy Ave.
Santa Fe Springs CA 90670
562-623-7150
Fax: 562-623-7160
International marketing for Green Star and Green Power machines. US distributor for Green Power machine and other health care products.

Teldon of Canada Ltd
7432 Fraser Park Drive
Burnaby BC V5J 5B9
604-436-0545
800-663-2212
Fax: 604-435-4862
Exclusive Canadian distributor of the Green Life and Green Power machines as well as other unique health care products.

For Health Care Products and Kitchen Supplies:

Health Force Regeneration Systems
PO Box 5005
Rancho Santa Fe CA 92067-5005
619-756-5292
800-357-2717
Sells their own recipe book, plus a wide variety of health care equipment and products.

Kyrocera
Ceramic Application Products
8611 Balboa Avenue
San Diego CA 92123
800-537-0294
For Zirconia Knives.

Perfect Health
5423 Driftwood Street
Oxnard CA 93035
805-382-2021 or 800-444-4584
Fax: 805-984-2780
Sells a wide variety of health care products including juicers, waterless cookware, dehydrators, books and exercise equipment.

Star Restaurant Supplies
6178 Sepulveda Blvd
Van Nuys CA 91411
818-887-1188
For a wide range of food preparation supplies including the commercial Vita-Mix and Swiss six-sided stainless steel grater.

The Wooden Spoon
PO Box 931
Clinton CT 06413-0931
800-421-2207
They have wonderful cookie cutters, wooden spoons and other delights to put in your kitchen.

Weavewood
7520 Wayzata Blvd.
Minneapolis, MN 55426
800-367-6460
The most elegant wooden bowls and plates, plus serving size bowls and platters, even dishwasher safe.

Health Centers:

Hippocrates Health Institute
1443 Palmdale Court
West Palm Beach FL 33411
800-842-2125
Offers retreats, health professional training programs - ask about their catalogue of health care items.

Optimum Health Institute
6970 Central Avenue
Lemon Grove CA 91945
800-993-4325
One to three week programs on living food, plus classes. Ask about their catalogue of health care supplies and equipment.

Tree of Life Rejuvenation Center
PO Box 1080
Patagonia AZ 85624
520-394-2520 or 800-720-2520
Fax: 520-394-2099
Alternative care medical practitioner Dr. Gabriel Cousens offers living food programs and weekend retreats.

Food Resources

Organic Foods:

Diamond Organics
PO Box 2159
Freedom CA 95019
408-763-1993 or 800-922-2396
Fax: 800-290-3683 or 408-763-2444
For their free catalogue, listing the widest selection of organically grown vegetables, fresh cut flowers, dried fruits and nuts, pastas and breads, and olive oil, with no minimum order needed.

Gold Mine Natural Food
7805 Arjons Drive
San Diego CA 92126–4368
(858)-537-9830
Toll Free 1-800-475-3663
Fax: (858) 695-0811
www.goldminenaturalfood.com
For a catalogue of their naturally and organically grown foods including hull-less barley, beans, seeds, rice, sea vegetables, herb teas, cookware and other kitchen and home items. No minimum order necessary.

(The) Grain & Salt Society
273 Fairway
Asheville NC 28805
828-299-9005
Fax: 828-299-1640
Web: celtic-seasalt.com
Celtic Salt distributor, lovely salt boxes and jars, plus other macrobiotic foods and supplies. Ask about their newsletter.

Hygia Enterprises
2422 Hutchison Street
Vista CA 92084-1706
760-630-8288
Tomato Tornado and Popcorn Pizzazz - organically grown, dehydrated spices.

Jaffee Brothers Natural Foods
PO Box 636
Valley Center CA 92082
619-749-1133
Fax: 619-749-1282
For a catalogue of their full line of organically grown fruits, nuts, nut butters, beans, salad oils and other organic foods. No minimum order needed.

Johnny Selected Seeds
4 Fourth Hill Road
Albion Maine 04910
207 437-9294
Fax: 207 437-2165
For their catalogue of organically grown seeds, herbs and other products.

Main Coast Sea Vegetables
3 Georges Pond Road
Franklin ME 04634
207-565-2907
Supplies kelp, sea vegetable, nori and more.

Sun Organic Farms
P.O. Box 2429
Valley Centre CA 92082
888-269-9888
The best assortment of organic nuts, seeds, dried fruit, etc. Call and ask for their catalogue of goodies. Specialize in grains that are difficult to find - oats and barley that sprout. A reliable source of uncooked coconut and raw carob powder.

Walnut Acres
PO Box 8
Penns Creek Pennsylvania 17862
800-433-3998
Fax: 717-873-1146
For their free catalogue, includes nuts, seeds, condiments, and an array of fresh organic vegetables. No minimum order necessary.

Wysong
1880 North Eastman Road
Midland Michigan 48640
800-748-0188
Fax: 517-631-8801
For their free catalogue of organically grown dried fruits, herbs, beans, nuts and nut butters and other food products. No minimum order necessary.

Curries:

Blue Mountain Jamaican Curry: a mild curry available at specialty stores or
AKKA Market
4233 Crenshaw Blvd
Los Angeles CA 90008
213-292-8921 or 909-397-0647

Instant India products: one of the best curry pastes available from **East India Company**
Phone or fax: 210-521-9112

Salty Spices:

Most of these salty spices are available at your local natural food store, taste and decide which you prefer:

Bragg's Liquid Aminos: a soy based product, like soy sauce, not fermented, no unnecessary preservatives.

163

Food Resources

Celtic Salt: available in health food stores or from The Grain & Salt Society (see Organic Foods).

Miso: a soy bean paste, very salty, used for soups, sauces, many different kinds, the yellow and white are sweeter, the barley, rice and soy are stronger, saltier. Be sure to buy in the refrigerator section, although fermented there are live enzymes in this food.

Mrs. Dash: available in different flavors, found in most markets.

Shoyu or Wheat-free Tamari: organic and not genetically altered soy sauce made by SanJ.

Other Choices:

Dr. Bronner's Minerals – soy, vegetable combination

Dr. Jensen's Quick Sip – soy, vegetable combination

Spike – salt, or unsalted, plus vegetable seasonings

Sesame Salt/Gomasio – toasted sesame seeds and salt

Special Foods:

Bok Choy: a crisp green leafy plant, with a white middle stalk, very water rich

Flax Seeds: very high in Omega 3 and 6 oils, essential fatty acids, available in most natural food stores.

Jicama: looks like a rock, very sweet, very crisp, like a sweet white carrot

Oat Groats: the whole oat, not a flake or rolled oats

Tomato Products:

Tomato Pesto: a mixture of organic dried tomatoes, garlic and olive oil, made by Trader Joes.

Tomatillos: a green tomato like fruit, covered in its own 'cocoon,' very tart, excellent blended with other vegetables or as its own sauce.

Tomato Tornado: an organic dried tomato powder spice, excellent on salads, squash, many vegetables, order it from Hygia Enterprises.

These resources are compliments of:

Elysa Markowitz
The Raw & Wild Food Lady
TV host of Elysa's Raw & Wild Food Show

For recipes books, catalogues of her TV shows on VHS or to discuss giving food demonstrations, dinners or workshops call, write or fax:

17551 Mountain View Road Suite 47
Desert Hot Springs CA 92240
Telephone: 760-251-7488
Fax: 760-288-4595
www.galaxymall.com/health/livingfoods
email: elysatv@earthlink.net

Recommended Reading

Agriculture by Rudolf Steiner
Amazing Grains by J. Saltzman
Diet for a New America by John Robbins
Food as Medicine by Dr. Earl Mindell
Gardening for Health and Nutrition by John and Helen Philbrick
Healing with Food by Mervyn Webach
Healing with Herbal Juices by Siegfried Gursche (2nd edition)

Intuitive Eating by H. Santillo
Joy of Juicing by G. and S. Null
Make Your Juicer Your Drugstore by L. Newman
Moosewood Restaurant Kitchen Garden by D. Hirsch
Raw Energy by Leslie Kenton
Recipes for Longer Life by Ann Wigmore
Super Nutrition Gardening by W. S Perry and W. Peary
Ten Day Clean Up Plan by Leslie Kenton

Bibliography

Appleton, Nancy. 1988, *Lick the Sugar Habit*. Garden City Park, NY: Avery.

Baker, Elizabeth. 1981, *The Uncook Book: Raw Food Adventure to a New Health High*. Indianola, WA: Drelwood Communications.

Blauer, Stephen. 1989. *The Juicing Book*. Garden City, NY: Avery.

Cousens, Gabriel. 1992. *Conscious Eating*. Santa Rosa, CA: Vision Books International.

Diamons, Harvey and Marilyn. 1985. *Fit for Life*. New York, NY: Warner Books.

Graham, Douglas. 1991. *The High Energy Diet Recipe Guide*. Trinidad: H.E.M Printers.

Haas, Elson M. 1981. *Staying Healthy with the Seasons*. Berkeley, CA: Celestial Arts.

Howell, Edward. 1985. *Enzyme Nutrition*. Wayne, NJ: Avery Publishing Group.

Hunt, Charles J. 1992. *The Christ Diet*. La Jolla, CA: Heartquake Publishing.

Kirschman, John. D. 1975. *Nutrition Almanac*. McGraw Hill Books.

Levin, James and Natalie Cederquist. 1993. *Vibrant Living*. San Diego, CA: GLO, Inc.

Santillo, Humbart. 1991. *Food Enzymes – The Missing Link To Radiant Health*. Prescott, Arizona: Hohm Press.

Sproul, Kim and Jamey Dina. 1991. *Uncooking with Jamey and Kim*. San Diego, CA: self-published.

Walker, Norman. 1970. *Fresh Vegetable and Fruit Juices*. Prescott, Arizona: Norwalk Press.

Walker, Norman. 1976. *Raw Vegetable and Fruit Juices*. A Pyramid Book.

About the Author

Elysa Markowitz, television host of *Elysa's Raw and Wild Food Show* seen coast to coast has been a nationally known and respected speaker in the health care field for over 20 years. Since 1991, she has traveled around the United States presenting at national health conferences and has been well received by audiences who delight in her enthusiasm, knowledge and personal flair for preparing raw food dishes.

Formerly the Director of Baby Dance Institute, she comes to this field with a rich and eclectic background: as a Department Chairwoman of Perinatal Health Education at Hollywood Presbyterian Medical Center and with her bachelors degree in Perinatal Health Education—she has lectured to thousands of couples each year about the importance of starting a family with a healthy baby. Her innovative approach to education is acclaimed by health care providers Dr. Gabriel Cousens and Dr. Michael Klapper. Both endorse her programs and enjoy eating her exciting new cuisine.

She loves to teach and enjoys sharing what she learns from life and others. She is the author of *Baby Dance: A Comprehensive Guide to Prenatal and Postpartum Exercises, Food for Thought: Elysa's Private Recipe Collection* and *Warming Up to Living Foods*. She also wrote and appeared in an educational CPR video – *How to Save Your Child's Life*. She is currently living and writing in the southwestern US and travels the North America giving workshops. She loves to play with her food and inspires others to do the same.

Recipe and Ingredient Index

Encyclopedia *of* Natural Healing - Alive Research Group

The most comprehensive self-help guide to natural health published in North America. Lists more than 300 conditions, with symptoms, causes, herbal treatments, nutritional supplements, homeopathy and external therapies for each.

Everything you need to heal yourself and your family - naturally.

Winner of the Benjamin Franklin Award for excellence

1,472 pages, hardcover, with 1,200 colour photos and illustrations

$69.95 Cdn • $59.95 US   ISBN 0-920470-75-0

Best-Sellers

Best-Sellers

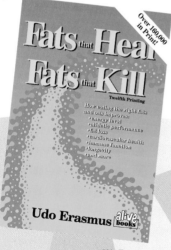

Carolee Bateson-Koch DC ND
212 pages - Softcover

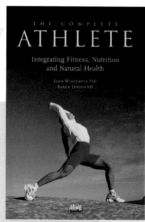

John Winterdyk PhD, Karen Jensen ND
320 pages - Softcover

Rudolph Breuss
114 pages - Softcover

Udo Erasmus
480 pages - Softcover

Naomi Shannon
219 pages - Softcover w/French Flaps
Lavishly illustrated and full colour throughout.

Dagmar von Cramm
240 pages - Softcover w/French Flaps
Lavishly illustrated and full colour throughout.

Alive Publishing has been motivating and supporting people

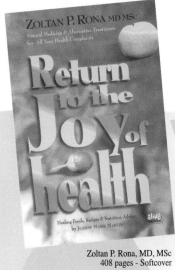

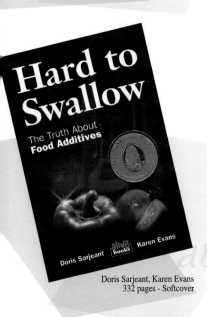
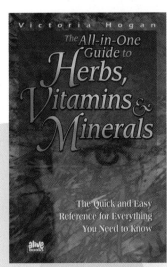
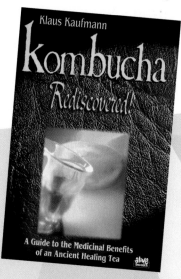
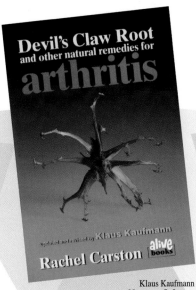
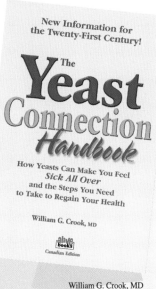

Natural Health Guides

Your best source of health and nutrition information.

Look for the full series at your local health food store, nutrition centre or bookstore.
Find your closest health food store at *www.alivepublishing.com*.

Self-Help Information

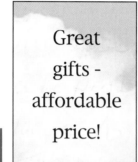

Great gifts - affordable price!

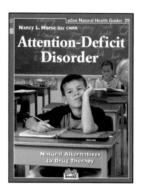

alive Natural Health Guides 29
Nancy L. Morse BSc CNPA
Attention-Deficit Disorder
Natural Alternatives to Drug Therapy

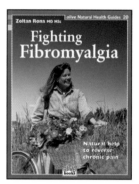

alive Natural Health Guides 20
Zoltan Rona MD MSc
Fighting Fibromyalgia
Natural help to reverse chronic pain

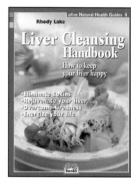

alive Natural Health Guides 4
Rhody Lake
Liver Cleansing Handbook
How to keep your liver happy
•Eliminate toxins
•Rejuvenate your liver
•Overcome tiredness
•Energize your life

alive Natural Health Guides 8
William G. Crook PhD
Nature's Own Candida Cure
Powerful remedies to combat yeast-related health disorders

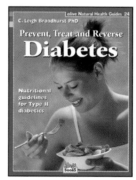

alive Natural Health Guides 24
C. Leigh Broadhurst PhD
Prevent, Treat and Reverse
Diabetes
Nutritional guidelines for Type II diabetics

alive Natural Health Guides 16
Zoltan Rona MD
Osteoarthritis
Treat and reverse joint pain naturally

alive Natural Health Guides 26
Zoltan Rona MD MSc
Rheumatoid Arthritis
Decrease or reverse symptoms naturally

Expert authors • Easy-to-read information • Tasty recipes

Healing Foods & Herbs

alive Natural Health Guides 28
C. Leigh Broadhurst PhD
Health and Healing with Bee Products
Boost health, treat conditions and prevent disease with:
•Bee Pollen
•Propolis
•Honey
•Royal Jelly

alive Natural Health Guides 10
Phyllis I. Dales and Bruce Dales
Cranberry
The Cure for Common and Chronic Conditions
•Urinary Tract Infection
•Eye disorder and others

alive Natural Health Guides 6
Nancy L. Morse
Evening Primrose Oil
The healing power of the yellow flower
• PMS
• Menopause
• Skin problems
• and more

alive Natural Health Guides 30
Kathleen O'Bannon CNC
Sprouts
The savory source for health and vitality

alive Natural Health Guides 1
Siegfried Gursche
Fantastic Flax
A powerful defense against cancer, heart disease and digestive disorders

alive Natural Health Guides 14
Harald W. Tietze
Papaya
The Healing Fruit
Information, remedies and recipes for
• Improved digestion
• Skin conditions
• Cancer
• Boosting the immune system
• and much more

alive Natural Health Guides 31
Kathleen O'Bannon CNC
Whole Foods for Seniors
Feel Younger! Live Longer!

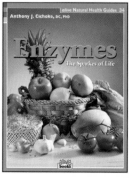

alive Natural Health Guides 34
Anthony J. Cichoke, DC, PhD
Enzymes
The Sparkes of Life

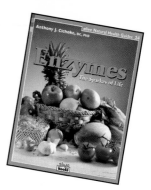
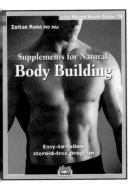

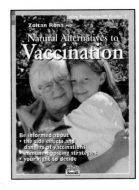
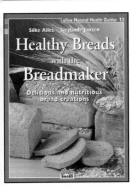

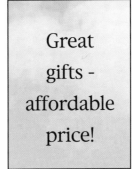

Notes

Guacamole mix
1 tomatos
1 Jalopino
1 Avacado
lime OR lemon Juice
Salt
Onions

Notes

Notes

Notes

Notes